# Hand-Applied Finishes

1043

# Hand-Applied Finishes

JEFF JEWITT

The Taunton Press

Cover photo: Scott Phillips

*for fellow enthusiasts*

First printing: 1997
Printed in the United States of America

A FINE WOODWORKING Book

FINE WOODWORKING® is a trademark of The Taunton Press, Inc.,
registered in the U.S. Patent and Trademark Office.

The Taunton Press, 63 South Main Street, Box 5506, Newtown,
CT 06470-5506

Library of Congress Cataloging-in-Publication Data

Jewitt, Jeff.
    Hand-applied finishes / Jeff Jewitt.
        p.    cm.
    "A Fine woodworking book."
    Includes index.
    ISBN 1-56158-154-2
    1. Wood finishing.        I. Title.
TT325.J42    1997
684'.084—dc20                                    96-43181
                                                   CIP

## About Your Safety

Working wood is inherently dangerous. Using hand or power tools improperly or
ignoring standard safety practices can lead to permanent injury or even death. Don't try
to perform operations you learn about here (or elsewhere) unless you're certain they are
safe for you. If something about an operation doesn't feel right, don't do it. Look for
another way. We want you to enjoy the craft, so please keep safety foremost in your mind
whenever you're in the shop.

To my wife, Susan

# Contents

# Acknowledgments

I'd like to thank several people who provided assistance with technical information as I was preparing this book. Their names are listed by chapter.

Monona Rossol, for health and safety information (Chapter 1).

Chris Minick and Larry Cavalier, for technical information on abrasives (Chapter 2).

Mark Williams at Veritas Tools, for help with the section on scrapers (Chapter 2).

Chris Minick and Dr. Mark Van Dress, for technical assistance with drying-oil chemistry (Chapter 5).

Jay Hawkins, for information on varnish history (Chapter 6).

Jonathan Kemp and Pat Devine, for information on padding lacquers (Chapter 7).

Dr. Mark Van Dress and Chris Minick for sharing their technical expertise with water-based-finish chemistry (Chapter 8).

I'm also grateful to Wayne Dustman, who made the elegant comb-back Windsor chair shown in the photos in Chapter 9.

This book would not have been possible without the help, encouragement, and support of my wife, Susan. Her input has been so great that her name rightfully belongs on the front cover with mine.

Finally, I'd like to thank three other people: Peter Chapman, my editor at The Taunton Press, and Ernie and Susan Conover. Ernie took all the photos for this book, and it was on his and Susan's insistence that I wrote the book in the first place. Thanks Conovers!

# Introduction

Although many books and articles have been written on the subject, finishing remains one of the biggest bugaboos for woodworkers. Three years ago I began teaching a course called "Six Finishes in Two Days." The idea behind the course was to omit some of the theory and chemistry of finishing and simply to demonstrate six classic finishes from beginning to end using actual products and projects. Although some students are interested in the whys and hows of finish chemistry, most just want to learn how to finish.

This book evolved naturally from the finishing course. It is intended to be a reference manual of techniques for applying finishes to wood by hand. Most people erroneously assume that flawless finishes are sprayed on or that there is some "trick" to achieving superb results. This is simply not true. Flawless finishes have been produced for hundreds of years using simple tools like brushes and pads. This book takes you through the process of applying different kinds of finishes, detailing each process, the materials used, and the correct technique.

The book is organized according to the natural sequence of finishing. Starting with the basics of material selection, the chapters progress from surface preparation and coloring to the actual process of applying the finishing material. Since all finishing materials vary in characteristics, the methods for applying them are slightly different. Each technique is accompanied by photos and a step-by-step text so that you can grasp the application nuances.

I've tried to present as many application options as possible for each type of finish. If you're a beginner or novice, you'll find this approach better suited to your skills and the materials you have access to. If you're more advanced, you'll find alternate techniques to improve your skills.

# 1

# Getting Started

Finishing begins well before you pick up a can of stain or a brush. Everything you do from initial design to final assembly affects the outcome of the finish. For example, how well you lay out and dimension stock determines how easy it is to sand it. How well you glue up a dovetailed drawer affects the staining and finishing. Equally important is the environment in which you apply the finish.

## The Right Environment

When a finish fails, it's natural to blame the finish or your own application skills. But many finishes fail simply because they are applied in an unsuitable environment. Finishes are complex chemical products that react differently to extremes of temperature and humidity. Inability to dry, "blushing," and "bleeding" are all attributable to extreme weather conditions and improper ventilation (see the Glossary at the back of the book for definition of finishing terms). Lighting is another easily overlooked area; improper lighting makes it difficult to detect missed glue spots, small dents, or uneven finish application, and makes accurate color matching nearly impossible. Dust is yet another problem, especially with slow-drying finishes like varnish.

A backlight positioned directly behind the surface you're working on is a great help when brushing on a finish.

A big step in controlling the quality of finishes, then, is to maintain a suitable environment in which they are applied. There are several simple and effective steps that can be taken to maintain temperature, increase ventilation, remove vapors and dust, and improve lighting. An added benefit is that not only will your finishes improve, but you'll also be much healthier for it.

## TEMPERATURE

All finishes are sensitive to application in extremes of temperature. Not only is the cure time affected, but application also becomes difficult, if not impossible, in extreme situations. With most finishes, heat is not as big a problem as cold, as long as it's dry heat. Most finishes cure more rapidly in high heat, but, unless you live in the desert, higher temperatures usually mean higher humidity, which poses a problem that we'll cover shortly (see p. 4).

Cold can have a variety of effects, depending on the finishing material. Cold finishes are harder to apply and do not flow out and level properly if brushed. They cure very slowly, if at all, when the air is below 60°F. Oil-based reactive finishes (those that dry by reacting with oxygen in the air, such as varnish and linseed oil) take longer to cure in cold conditions and at low enough temperatures refuse to cure at all. Solvent-release finishes like lacquer and shellac aren't as fussy in cure time in extremes of temperature but won't flow out properly if applied by brush below 65°F. Water-based finishes are the most finicky in cold weather, and problems are likely at temperatures below 65°F. The ideal air temperature for applying finishes is 70°F to 80°F. The finish and the object being finished should also be maintained within this range. In short, don't use cold finishes and don't put finishes on cold wood.

You can use heaters to warm cold workshop areas, but there are a couple of important things to bear in mind. If you use a wood-burning stove or other open-flame heating, your finishing options are limited and the area in which you work should be as far away from the source of heat as possible. The greatest risk is from the buildup of flammable vapors, which could possibly ignite when a heater kicks on. When working in a small basement room, open the doors and provide adequate ventilation when using flammable materials.

## RELATIVE HUMIDITY

Relative humidity (RH) is defined as the amount of moisture in the air compared to the amount of moisture it is capable of holding. It is expressed as a percentage, and its effects on finishes are problematic when it is very high. Oil-based reactive products are generally not affected by high RH, but cure time can be increased. Solvent-release finishes fare much worse. In 90% RH and above, shellac and lacquer may turn white, or "blush," after application. Blushing can be remedied by adding a retarder to slow down the evaporation, but it's usually better to wait until the RH drops. Water-based finishes have problems in RH above 80%. The most noticeable problem is slow dry time, given that these finishes contain water as the carrier. When the air is already holding a lot of moisture, it won't want to take on any more. In extreme cases (above 95% RH), the coalescing solvent evaporates before the water does; as a result, the finish will not form a smooth, contiguous film.

Because temperature and relative humidity are so critical to proper finishing, it's a good idea to invest in a thermometer/ hygrometer. An inexpensive digital model is available from Radio Shack (catalog #63-867).

## LIGHTING

Lighting is not as critical to a quality finish as temperature and relative humidity, but an effort should be made to provide as good a light source as possible. Proper lighting is necessary to show defects in sanded surfaces. Good lighting also helps you see whether you've applied finish evenly, particularly when brushing. In most cases, the optimum lighting is ambient (indirect) natural daylight from windows and skylights, but for some operations you need backlighting. A gooseneck lamp clamped to a bench usually suffices (see the photo on p. 3).

If you work in an area without windows, the type of artificial lighting you choose is very important. Incandescent (regular lightbulb) lighting is not a good choice for finishing if you do any color matching because it makes colors appear redder (warmer) than they really are. Incandescent lights also produce bright spots. Fluorescent lights are a better choice because the light is produced by a large tube, which does not throw harsh shadows and results in more even lighting. Purchase neutral lamps with a color temperature of 4,200 Kelvin. Although they are more expensive, these lamps have the best overall color rendition and simulate natural daylight best.

## DUST

Dust is the inevitable by-product of woodworking operations; you create it every time you cut, rout, sand, or drill. Finishes and dust do not mix, but there are several things you can do to alleviate dust problems in the finish. If space allows, set up a separate room for finishing. If you have to finish in the same room as you do your surface preparation, wait a day or so (at least overnight) after sanding. Either way, use source dust collectors on all machines, particularly on sanding equipment. The fine dust created by these machines will infiltrate everywhere. Varnishes are the most susceptible to dust. Apply varnish at the end of the day, so that you won't be walking around the shop kicking up dust. In some situations, the best solution is to use fast-drying finishes that don't give dust a chance to settle. These finishes include shellac, solvent lacquer, and water-based lacquer, which dry to the touch in a matter of minutes.

Don't become so obsessed with dust that you tear out your hair every time a speck lands in the middle of your freshly brushed varnish. The best-looking finishes are rubbed out—a process that levels the dried finish and removes small imperfections like dust. (Rubbing out is discussed at length in Chapter 6.)

## Personal Safety

Finishing products are made up of complex chemical products. Many of these contain organic solvents that are flammable, irritating to lungs and skin, and harmful or poisonous if swallowed. In short, they are bad for you, and you need to take appropriate precautions to protect yourself. You also need to protect yourself from fine wood dust created during the sanding process and from noise generated by high-pitched sanders and vacuums.

## SOLVENTS

Almost all the products used as finishing materials contain organic solvents. These solvents are divided into groups; the most common in finishing are hydrocarbons (mineral spirits), chlorinated hydro-carbons (methylene chloride), alcohols (methanol, ethanol), glycol ethers (coalescing solvents used in water-based finishes), esters (lacquer solvents), and ketones (acetone, lacquer thinner).

All solvents differ in degrees of hazard (for example, ethanol is far less toxic than methanol), but all enter the body through either the lungs or the skin. For best respiratory protection, work in a well-ventilated room (see p. 7). When applying finish to a large area or working in close proximity to solvent-laden varnishes and lacquers, wear an organic-vapor cartridge-style respirator for added protection. These respirators must fit correctly to be effective. I recommend that you buy a respirator from one of the major safety-supply companies (such as Mine Safety Appliance Co., P.O. Box 426, Pittsburgh, PA 15230; 800-672-2222). These companies have staff experienced in selling the correct-style mask and cartridge for your needs and also carry test kits to determine correct fit. Change your respirator's cartridges and prefilters on a regular basis—don't wait until you smell solvent through the filters.

Gloves are recommended when handling any solvent; even the relatively nontoxic solvents like ethanol can dry out the skin. Wear "chemical-splash" goggles for eye protection and an apron to protect against spills. Use common sense when working with any finishing product. If something makes you sneeze, cough, or feel dizzy, stop what you're doing and get some fresh air. It should go without saying that you should always read the handling and safety warnings on the products you use.

## WOOD DUST

The hazards of wood dust are clearly established. Breathing fine wood dust such as that created by sanding is an irritant to the lungs. Fine airborne dust stays suspended in the air, while heavier dust particles fall to the floor. When machining and sanding wood and composite wood products like plywood and particleboard, use a dust collector at the source and wear a dust mask rated for fine particulates.

## NOISE

Noise is measured by a decibel rating, and, at certain levels, hearing protection is advised. Sanding machines, canister vacuums, and dust collectors create the most harmful noise, and appropriate

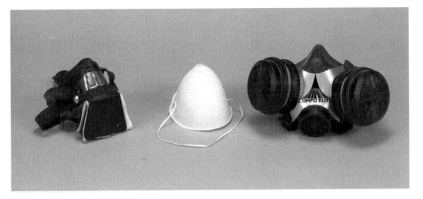

The quarter-mask respirator on the left is designed for use with fine particulates, while the "nuisance" mask in the center will block only large particulates. An organic-vapor respirator (right) is recommended when working with solvent-laden varnishes and lacquers.

hearing protection should be worn when using them. I find earmuff-type protectors the most comfortable, but other styles are available that provide just as good protection.

## Workshop Safety

The area most often neglected in controlling the safe use of finishing products is the finishing room itself. Most finishing products can be used safely without risk of fire and explosion only if proper handling, storage, and disposal of these products are followed.

Flammable and hazardous finishing materials should always be stored in a metal cabinet (see the photo at right). If shop design permits, I recommend venting the cabinet at the top and ducting it outside to prevent the buildup of solvent vapors within the cabinet.

Proper ventilation removes solvent-laden air from the shop and is necessary for proper drying of finishing materials. Cross-ventilation—an influx of fresh air and an exhaust of shop air—provides the best protection for the woodworker and reduces the buildup of hazardous vapors (see the drawing on p. 8). Applying finishes by hand (rather than by sprayer) greatly reduces any potentially dangerous buildup of vapors, but a window exhaust fan is still a good idea. Keep a door open to bring in fresh air. A fan can be placed so that it blows air toward an open door, but keep it from blowing directly over a wet finish, which could cause flowout and leveling problems.

Most small shops do not generate enough hazardous material to be regulated, so proper disposal is the responsibility of the user. Never pour finishing materials down the drain. Set them outside where the solvents (even water-based) can evaporate, and then dispose of the dry resin as you would any garbage. If you are

For safety, finishing materials should be stored in a metal cabinet.

## CROSS-VENTILATION

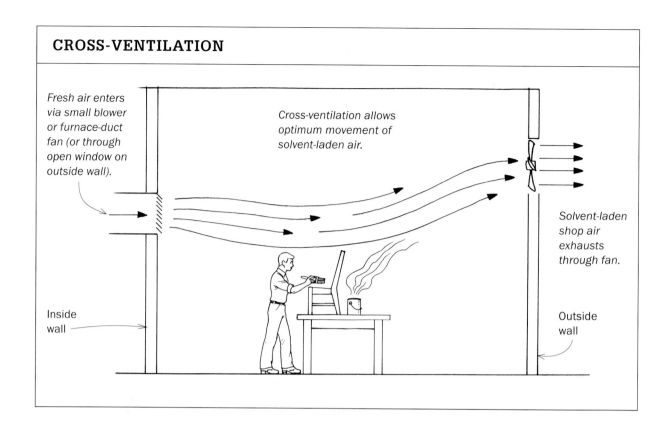

Fresh air enters via small blower or furnace-duct fan (or through open window on outside wall).

Cross-ventilation allows optimum movement of solvent-laden air.

Solvent-laden shop air exhausts through fan.

Inside wall

Outside wall

**To reduce the risk of fire, store oily rags in a specially designed disposal pail.**

concerned about putting the dried material in the garbage, call your municipal waste-treatment facility for advice.

Many finishing items can be recycled for other finishing tasks. Rags used for light cleaning and rubbing out can be cleaned and used for removing glaze and cleaning stripping residue. Thinners used for cleaning can be used to clean off stripped furniture. Oily rags pose a very hazardous problem and must be disposed of properly. Oil-soaked rags can combust spontaneously and start a fire. The risk of fire is greatest when the rags are balled up and thrown in with other combustible items such as wood and paper. The chemical reaction that causes the oil to cure produces enough heat to start a fire. To reduce the risk of fire, dispose of rags in a specially designed container (available from industrial safety suppliers). Empty the container at the end of the day, run the rags under cold water, and then dispose of them. Alternatively, soak rags in water, then drape them over the side of a metal trash can to dry.

Every shop should have at least one fire-extinguisher. Check with your supplier for the type rated for extinguishing organic solvents.

# Finishing Tools

When a finish doesn't turn out right, it's often because the wrong finishing tool was used. You don't need sophisticated tools to apply finishes by hand, but you do need to know which applicator to use. The three basic types of finishing tools are brushes, cloth pads, and applicator pads.

## BRUSHES

Brushes are the most common finishing tool, available in hundreds of different styles that vary in shape, size, bristle, and cost. Choosing the right brush is as important as choosing the right finish (see the sidebar on p. 14).

***Brush construction***   All brushes have the same basic components: bristles, setting, divider, ferrule, and handle (see the drawing at right). The *bristles,* which can be either natural hair or synthetic filament, take up, hold, and release the finish to the work when brushing. The *setting* is a glue, usually epoxy, that holds the butt end of the bristles in place. *Dividers* are wooden plugs placed into the setting that create a reservoir and determine the shape of the brush. One or two dividers are used depending on the thickness of the brush. Dividers are omitted in artist's brushes and some specialty brushes. A *ferrule* is a metal band in which the setting is anchored and attached to the handle. The *handle,* which is usually a hardwood like beech, determines the comfort of a brush; it can be "beaver-tailed" for good balance and less fatigue, or long and thin for precise control.

A well-made brush with quality components is an indispensable tool and a pleasure to use. Of all the components, none is more critical for finishing performance than the bristle. Bristle technically refers to a specific type of animal hair, but in brush manufacture it is a generic term. Bristle is subdivided into two main classes: natural hair and synthetic filament.

***Natural-hair brushes***   Natural-hair brushes are further subdivided into two categories, soft fur and hog bristle. Soft fur comes from animals like weasels, mink, badgers, and oxen. Soft-fur brushes are typically artist's brushes and some of the specialty brushes. Hog bristle is the hair from hogs and is commonly used in painting and finishing brushes. Many times, two or more hair types are mixed to produce brushes with specific performance characteristics.

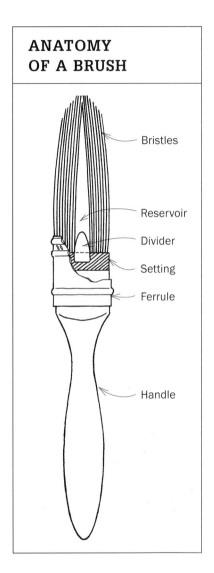

**ANATOMY OF A BRUSH**

- Bristles
- Reservoir
- Divider
- Setting
- Ferrule
- Handle

The best bristle comes from Chinese hogs and is either white or black in color. *Hog bristle* has two distinct advantages over other types of hair. It is naturally tapered toward the tip and has flags or split ends at the tip. The taper gives bristle resilience and spring; the flags allow heavier loading of finish material at the tip.

*Sable* is the best natural hair for artist's brushes because it forms a fine sharp point when wet. Kolinsky sable from the mink is the best; other sables are made from weasels.

*Camel* is actually a misnomer since the hair is not from camels but from the tails of European squirrels. Camel-hair brushes are often used for lettering and detail work.

*Ox* hair, taken from behind the ears of oxen, is silky and durable. Ox-hair brushes are used extensively in sign painting.

*Badger,* a very soft and resilient hair, is regarded as one of the best hairs for flowing on finishes like oil varnishes and lacquer. It does not have the body of hog bristle, so it is usually combined with other hairs such as bristle or skunk.

*Fitch* is a somewhat confusing term because it applies both to a type of hair and to a specific brush. American fitch is from a skunk, whereas European fitch is from a gray or black weasel. Fitch brushes are made from skunk, badger, or bristle, or from a combination of these three hairs.

**Synthetic-filament brushes**   The distinct advantage of synthetic filament over natural hair is that synthetic filament absorbs only 7% of its weight in water. Natural hair absorbs 100% of its weight, causing it to become floppy and soft in water-based finishes. Modern machinery is now able to duplicate the flags on synthetic filaments so that synthetics are the best choice for water-based products. Chinex is the most recent filament developed and is excellent for all water-based paints and finishes. Taklon is a generic term for artist's brushes made from tapered nylon; these are excellent brushes for applying shellac and lacquer. Because of their rectangular chisel edge, Taklon brushes are useful where precise control is needed.

**Bristle configuration**   The different brush profiles are shown in the drawing on the facing page. Natural and synthetic brushes are available in flat trim, rectangular chisel, and oval chisel. The bristle can be blunt end (or "square cut"), flagged, or tapered. Flat-trim brushes are usually square cut; they are useful in exterior painting because the blunt tip of the bristle can work the paint into the

## BRUSH PROFILES AND BRISTLE TYPES

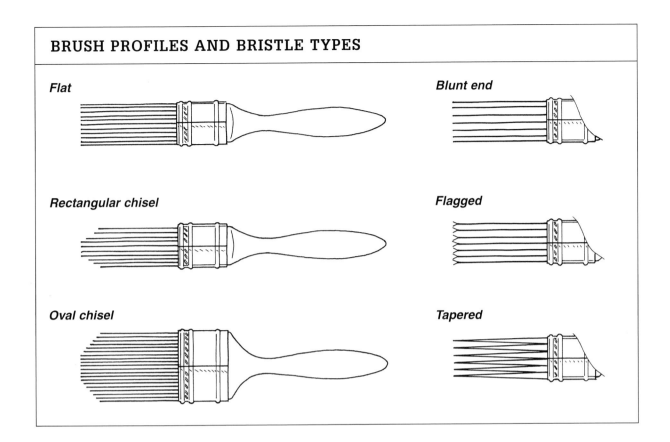

**Flat**

**Blunt end**

**Rectangular chisel**

**Flagged**

**Oval chisel**

**Tapered**

crevices of the wood. The chisel edge on rectangular and oval brushes is preferred for its ability to "cut in," or draw a straight even line. The bristle on these brushes is either flagged or very fine, which makes them the best brushes for all finishing work, whether you're finishing a flat top or a complex edge. Tapered bristles are found on synthetic-filament artist brushes; the fine ends leave less noticeable brush marks than the thicker filament found on blunt-end bristles.

**Caring for a brush**   A brush that is properly cared for should improve with use. Before using a brush, tap the bristles against a table or your palm to dislodge any debris or loose bristle. Then dip the brush in the thinner for the material you're using. Use alcohol for shellac, mineral spirits for oil-based products, and water for water-based products. Dipping the brush in thinner makes it much easier to clean when you're through. Remove excess thinner by wrapping the bristles in a rag, and then dip the brush into the finish.

When you're ready to clean the brush, brush the excess finish on some newspaper and dip the brush into the appropriate thinner. Scrape the brush across the lip of a metal can to remove excess thinner. Apply a liberal amount of dishwashing detergent to the brush, and then lather the bristles with water by swirling the brush around in your cupped palm (see the photos below and at left on the facing page). Bend the bristles back to force finish out of the base near the ferrule, and then rinse with plenty of water. Repeat until the bristles no longer feel slimy. Next twirl the brush between the palms of your hands to spin out excess water. To keep the bristles shaped, comb them with a brush comb, and then wrap the brush in a paper towel or clean rag and lay it flat to dry (see the photo at right on the facing page).

Artist's brushes should be cleaned with soap and water as explained above, but after rinsing with water, dry the brush with a paper towel and then dip the tip into a 1-lb. cut shellac solution (see p. 72). Form the hairs or filament back into a fine point or chisel edge with your fingers and set the brush aside to dry. The

## Cleaning a Brush

**1. After rinsing the brush in the appropriate thinner, pour a generous amount of dishwashing detergent over the bristles.**

shellac sizes the brush and keeps the brush profile sharp. Soak the brush for a few minutes in alcohol before using.

If a brush has hardened finish in the bristles, soak it for several hours in an NMP (n-methyl 2-pyrrolidone) based stripper like Citristrip or Woodfinisher's Pride. Don't use a methylene-chloride-based stripper—it will destroy the stiffness of the bristle. Scrub the base of the bristles near the ferrule with a stiff wire brush to remove any softened finish, and then clean the brush as explained previously.

## CLOTHS

For applying wipe-on, wipe-off finishes and stains, almost any absorbent cloth can be used as long as it's lint-free and clean. Old clothes and diapers will work, provided they have been washed first and dried to remove lint. Paper towels are fine. For applying shellac and varnishes that are not wiped off completely, it's a good idea to use cloths with special weaves; these cloths will be dealt with in later chapters. If you use a lot of rags, consider purchasing them in bulk

2. Work the soap into the bristles by scrubbing them into the palm of your hand.

3. Once the brush is clean, wrap the bristles in a paper towel or clean rag and lay the brush flat to dry.

# Buying a Brush

A good-quality brush always performs better than a cheap one. When buying a brush, there are several features to look for. On chisel-tip brushes, check for flags on all the bristles, which indicate that the bristles are hand-cut. Rather than forming a chisel edge from bristles of various lengths, cheap brushes will have the chisel cut into the tip after the brush is made. These brushes can be identified by the lack of flags on the bristles.

Check for firmness of the bristle setting by tapping the brush against your hand. None of the bristles should fall out. Bend the bristles back and forth—they should feel springy. If you can pull the bristles far enough apart, check for an oversized divider. Manufacturers will sometimes use a large divider to give an illusion of fullness to the brush. The ferrule should be nickel-plated or stainless steel and should be firmly attached to the handle. Handles should feel balanced and comfortable in your hand. They can be finished or unfinished; unfinished handles are always used on brushes used in water-based products.

A basic brush inventory for finishing should include the following:

**Shellac** The fitch and the oval bristle are the best brushes for flowing on shellac. For quick application of shellac in thin coats, the 1½-in. Taklon works best.

**Oils and oil-based varnishes** An oval bristle with a chisel edge is my favorite, followed by the fitch brushes. A less expensive 100% white China bristle with a rectangular chisel edge also performs well. You'll need a 2-in. brush for finishing large surfaces and a 1-in. brush for cutting in.

**Solvent lacquer** Fitch and oval bristle brushes are recommended.

**Water-based products** Use only synthetic-bristle brushes—Chinex, Taklon, and Tynex are best. Flagged bristles work well for most products, but use a tapered synthetic bristle for products that tend to foam.

**Touchups and repairs** 100% red sable brushes are the only ones I recommend. At least two sizes, a #1 (for fine detail work) and a #4 (for larger areas), are needed.

**Among the author's favorite brushes for finishing are, from left to right, two rectangular China bristle brushes, three oval chisel bristle brushes, and two chisel-cut fitch brushes.**

from an industrial supplier. Look in the Business-to-Business Yellow Pages under "Wiping Cloths." Recommendations for various finishing operations are listed below.

*Staining:* Any absorbent cloth or paper towels.

*Grain filling:* Upholsterer's grade of burlap.

*Shellac:* Lint-free, open-weave "trace cloth" or padding cloth, surgical gauze.

*French polishing:* Traditionally, wool inside and linen for the outside of the pad. Absorbent cotton and muslin can be substituted.

*Wipe-on varnish and oils:* Lint-free, clean cotton cloth like diapers, T-shirt material, or padding cloth.

*Waxing and polishing:* Clean, bleached-cotton T-shirt type material. Cheesecloth or surgical gauze is good for buffing.

## APPLICATOR PADS

Applicator pads are very good at dispensing water-based stains and finishes quickly over a large area. They are less prone to foaming, a common problem when brushing water-based finishes, and can hold a great deal of finish before they need to be recharged. For finishing floors and large tables, they are the best choice. Just like paint-roller pads, applicator pads are available in various naps. Use the shortest nap you can find.

The downside of pads is that they work well only once or twice. They are hard to clean thoroughly, so I usually end up throwing them away after one session. I'm not fond of throwaway tools in principle, but they are fairly inexpensive to replace.

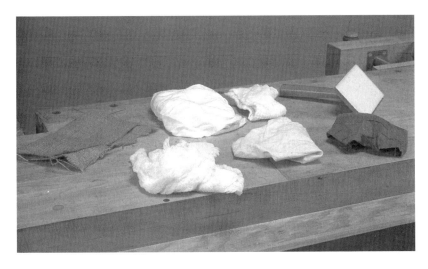

Cloths and pads used for finishing operations include (clockwise from left) burlap, T-shirt material, surgical gauze, an applicator pad, two types of muslin (one dyed, one bleached), and cheesecloth.

# 2

# Preparing the Wood

The two main reasons to apply finish to a wood surface are to protect it and to beautify it. However, when finishing materials are applied to wood with an uneven surface, machining marks, or other blemishes, they will exaggerate these defects, not cover them up. Surface preparation is necessary to flatten the stock, smooth the wood fibers, and correct other blemishes. It also provides a consistent surface so that subsequent staining and finishing products apply uniformly and adhere well.

## General Guidelines

Proper surface preparation is the first step in a well-executed finish, yet it is one of the most easily mishandled. To make surface preparation go smoothly and quickly, consider the following points before you pick up a belt sander or a scraper:
• *Use sharp cutting tools during machining.* Dull sawblades and router bits can cause burn marks that are hard to remove. Dull planer and jointer blades burnish wood fibers as they cut, which can result in stain-penetration problems—even if the wood is well sanded. Keep all your bits and blades sharp as you dimension and shape the individual parts to your project.
• *Prepare the parts before you glue.* Many woodworkers assume that surface preparation is something that starts only after the project is

**Using battens during panel glue-ups helps ensure board alignment and reduces the amount of surface preparation needed to level the panel.**

glued up and assembled. This way of thinking dooms a finish before you even start. Once a project is glued up, proper surface preparation is extremely time-consuming, if not impossible. It's much easier to prepare the individual parts to your project before gluing up; this way you can hold the parts securely and flat, which allows access to the entire surface area. Prepare all inside surfaces before you glue up. Leave all visible outside surfaces a bit rough to allow for later removal of dents and the inevitable clamp marks. Once the piece is assembled, a light sanding with fine sandpaper is usually all that's necessary before applying finishing materials.

• *Plan your glue-ups.* Improper gluing is one of the major causes of mistakes in subsequent finishing stages. Misaligned panels glued up from smaller pieces may need a lot of stock removal with a plane or belt sander to remove the ridges. Use battens to help ensure panel alignment (see the photo above). Gluing up on an uneven surface can put winds and twists into large panels, so make sure your glue table is flat. Glue squeeze-out is an insidious problem when applying stains and top coats (see the sidebar on p. 18). When gluing up, use pad clamps and put blankets on your glue-up table to prevent dents and scratches to the workpiece. Finally, allow several extra inches on each end of glued-up panels. When the panels are cut to size, these cutoffs are invaluable for testing stains and finishes for samples.

• *Choose your stock carefully.* Choose the best stock with the most consistent color and figure and put it on the outside, where it shows. Stock with dents, gouges, splits, knots, and sapwood can be arranged so that these defects are on backs or inside areas where they won't show. But if you have to or want to use defects on visible

# How to Avoid Glue Spots

There's nothing worse than finding a glue spot under the finish when you've completed a project. You'll avoid a lot of the headaches of glue spots by using proper gluing technique. Most woodworkers are satisfied that they've applied enough glue when they see a lot of glue squeeze-out when the joint is clamped, but the right amount of glue should produce only small beads around the clamped joint.

To dispense the right amount of glue on edge joints, use a glue roller bottle. Wipe off the excess glue with a wet rag, or wait until the glue is rubbery and then peel it off. Any glue residue can be sanded off during flattening and smoothing operations. On mortise-and-tenon joints, chamfer the ends of the tenon and around the mortise. Apply glue to the walls of the mortise and only to the leading edge of the tenon. If glue squeezes out, wait until it's rubbery and peel it off with your fingernail. On dovetails and other complex joints, use a sharp, profiled artist's brush to give you greater control when applying the glue. Using a white glue (like Elmer's) will give you more assembly time.

Hide glue isn't as noticeable if you get smears. Since hide glue is a protein, most dyes and finishes will penetrate to some degree but only if the glue spot is thin. Premixed hide glues have a long open time, and any excess can be wiped off with a wet rag. The hot glue made from granules has a short open time, but the excess will peel off like tape after several minutes.

Wiping PVA glue squeeze-out with a wet rag is not recommended, but if you must do it, use a clean, wet rag and follow immediately with a clean, dry rag. Letting the glue dry completely and trying to pop it off with a chisel is never recommended.

surfaces, see "Checking Surface Preparation" at the end of this chapter, which explains how to correct or stabilize these problems.

Surface preparation starts as soon as you begin your project, from the initial dimensioning right up to the application of the first coat of finish. By sticking to a planned schedule and doing surface preparation as you progress, you'll avoid a lot of the drudgery of flattening and smoothing. There are three main categories of tools for surface preparation—hand planes, scrapers, and abrasives—each of which leaves a slightly different surface on the wood.

## Hand Planes

The hand plane is one of the most useful tools for flattening and smoothing wood. Unlike its modern counterpart, the thickness planer, a bench plane produces a crisp, flawless surface ready for finishing. Planing wood requires a sharp blade and more skill in technique than scraping or sanding, but the results are well worth

Three hand planes that are essential for stock preparation are, from left to right, the jointer plane, the jack plane, and the block plane.

it. Planes come in hundreds of shapes and sizes, but there are three planes that are indispensable for surface preparation: the jointer plane, the jack plane, and the block plane.

The jointer plane has a long sole and is used primarily for jointing edges prior to edge gluing. With the blade crowned, it is an excellent tool for dressing rough stock and flattening large panels glued up from smaller stock. The blade is crowned so that it can make large, deep cuts. The long sole won't ride over variations in the surface of the wood, so it's best at leveling high spots in the stock.

The jack plane has a shorter sole than the jointer and can be used for rough dressing or final smoothing depending on how crowned the blade is. Fitted with a slightly crowned blade, the jack plane does an excellent job of smoothing. Fitted with a more pronounced crown, it is better suited for rough stock removal. Smoothing planes, which have a shorter sole than the jack, can also be used.

The block plane is my favorite plane for surface preparation. Top-quality models have an easy adjustment for changing the mouth opening for fine smoothing or rough shaping. A block plane is designed to be used with one hand so that the other hand can hold the stock. I use it for working small areas and detailing work, such as chamfering edges.

Using a plane to smooth wood is arguably one of the best ways to prepare the surface for finishing. A sharp plane blade severs the wood cleanly, leaving a surface that glistens slightly. Smoothing with a plane also leaves minor surface irregularities and evidence of hand workmanship that add a textural element under certain finishes. Unfortunately, hand planing can be accomplished correctly only by working with the grain of the wood, which in

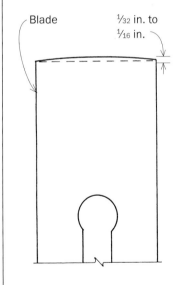

## CROWNED PLANE BLADE

*A blade with a crown of 1/32 in. to 1/16 in. is used for rough stock removal.*

Blade      1/32 in. to 1/16 in.

*For less aggressive cuts, reduce the crown to 1/64 in. or less.*

## PLANE AND SCRAPER SURFACES COMPARED

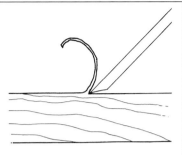

**Plane**

*A sharp plane blade severs fibers cleanly and leaves a smooth surface when working with the grain.*

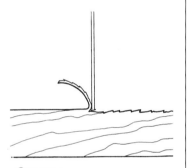

**Scraper**

*A scraper can be used against the grain, but its steep cutting angle leaves a ragged surface behind it if used to remove large shavings.*

some cases isn't possible. Hand planing can be difficult on highly figured woods and stock with knots unless you're very skilled and have the correct planes. Fortunately there is an alternative that works quite nicely—the scraper.

## Scrapers

Until sandpaper became widely available and affordable, virtually all woodworkers used scrapers. Scrapers fell into disuse for some while, but recently have made quite a comeback. The attraction of the tool is its simplicity and low cost, but it does take a bit of practice and skill to resharpen it. Mastering this tool is a very worthwhile goal for any woodworker.

The scraper gets its name from the way it is used to cut wood. Unlike the plane, which can cut large shavings from the wood, the scraper leaves a smooth surface only when it removes very thin shavings. If used to remove a large shaving, a very rough surface is the result (see the drawing at left).

Two types of scrapers are used to prepare wood. A hand scraper is simply a flat piece of hard steel that is meant to be held in both hands and either pushed or dragged across the wood to remove a shaving. It can be tilted slightly to adjust for optimum cutting action. Hand scrapers are available in a wide variety of shapes and thicknesses. Cabinet scrapers use a thicker piece of steel that is held in some type of wooden or metal body at a fixed angle. The body has a flat sole so it can level a surface just like a plane. Some of the more expensive designs have an adjustment to change the tilt of the blade to optimize the cutting action.

**Cabinet scrapers are available with adjustable-angle blades (left) and fixed blades (right).**

Like any other cutting tool, a scraper won't work properly unless it is sharpened correctly. Problems in using scrapers can usually be traced back to improper sharpening rather than to incorrect technique. There are as many ways to sharpen a scraper as there are ways to cut dovetails, but the goal is always the same—to produce a sharp hook, or "burr," to act as a cutting edge. On a hand scraper, the long edges of the steel are filed and honed so that they form a 90° angle to the sides. Then a burr is formed on the four edges; the burr is the cutting surface of the scraper. On a cabinet scraper, one edge is filed and honed to a 45° angle and a burr is drawn on that edge only.

Scrapers are sold in different hardness ratings based upon the Rockwell scale. If you're new to scrapers, buy one that is rated Rc 38–42 for ease of sharpening. Scrapers with special curved or

## SCRAPER HOLDER FOR SHARPENING

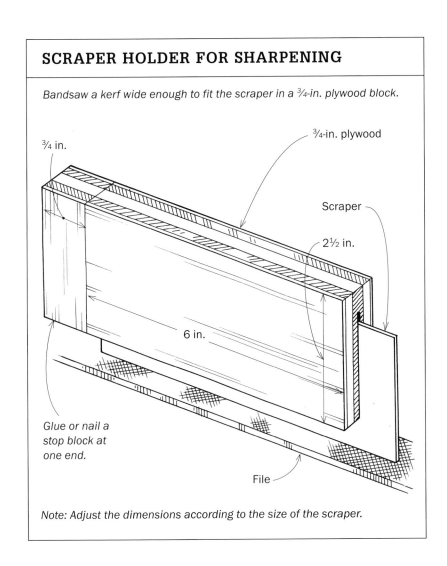

*Bandsaw a kerf wide enough to fit the scraper in a ¾-in. plywood block.*

¾ in.

¾-in. plywood

Scraper

2½ in.

6 in.

*Glue or nail a stop block at one end.*

File

*Note: Adjust the dimensions according to the size of the scraper.*

convex shapes are available for irregular-shaped pieces such as molding. These scrapers are sharpened just like the flat ones, although the curved edges take longer to prepare.

**SHARPENING A HAND SCRAPER**

Sharpening a hand scraper involves four steps: filing the edges, honing the edges, consolidating the edges, and drawing the burrs.

***Filing the edges*** Place a 10-in. single-cut mill file on a flat surface with the tang pointing away from you. A piece of wood or a bench dog works well as a stop. Hold the scraper at a 90° angle to the file and push it along the cutting length of the file several times (see the photo at left below). File until fresh metal is exposed along the entire length of the scraper. Turn the scraper over and do the other side, being careful not to cut yourself on the ragged burr. A block of wood with a kerf bandsawn into it will hold the scraper perfectly for this step (see the drawing on p. 21).

## Sharpening a Hand Scraper

1. To file the edge of a hand scraper, push the tool along the length of a file until fresh metal is exposed.

2. Hone the edge of the scraper on a fine-grit stone to remove the file marks.

# DRAWING A BURR ON A HAND SCRAPER

*A burnisher draws a burr at the edge of the scraper by pushing metal down in the shape of a hook.*

Burnisher

12° to 15°

Hand scraper

*Start with the burnisher at 90° to the face of the scraper, and then increase the angle slightly with each pass, stopping at about 12° to 15°.*

**3. Consolidate the edge of the scraper by drawing a round or teardrop-shaped burnisher along the edge.**

**4. With the scraper clamped securely in a vise, draw the burr by making a series of passes over the edge.**

**Honing the edges**   The file leaves a burr on the edges of the scraper, but the burr is too coarse to scrape wood without leaving a ragged surface. To smooth wood, the edges must be honed, just as a chisel or plane blade is honed after grinding the bevel. Using a fine-grit oilstone or an 800-grit waterstone and holding the scraper at 90°, make several passes to hone the edges (see the photo at right on p. 22). Flexing the scraper in the middle helps it ride at 90° to the stone and also prevents the blade from gouging the stone. Some people believe that honing up to grits as high as 6,000 creates a superior burr, but I haven't been able to discern a difference above 800 grit. Honing too much creates problems because it can round the edge, which will prevent you from rolling a good cutting burr. Lay the scraper flat on the stone and hone to remove the wire burr from filing.

**Consolidating the edges**   To consolidate the edges and draw the burrs you'll need a burnisher. You can buy a burnisher made specifically for scrapers or make one from round tool steel. Use either a round or teardrop-shaped burnisher and make sure the steel of the burnisher is harder than the steel of the scraper. Lay the scraper flat on a wooden surface about ⅛ in. in from the edge. Apply several drops of oil to the edge of the scraper, and then draw the burnisher along the edge of the scraper, starting parallel to the face and then gradually "rolling" the burnisher down a few degrees (see the photo at left on p. 23).

**Drawing the burrs**   To draw the burr, first clamp the scraper securely in a vise. Wipe one or two drops of oil on the burnisher, and then, holding the burnisher at a 90° angle to the face of the scraper, make one or two passes using light downward pressure. Next make a series of passes, gradually increasing the tilt of the burnisher until it reaches about 12° to 15° from perpendicular (see the photo at right on p. 23). With the scraper clamped in the same position, turn the burnisher around and do the other edge. Then flip the scraper to the opposite side and draw the burr on these two edges. The exact angle is approximate—there's no need to be precise since the scraper is tilted in operation to achieve optimum cutting.

## SHARPENING A CABINET SCRAPER

The general procedure for sharpening a cabinet scraper is the same as for a hand scraper, except that only one edge is sharpened and the goal is to produce a *beveled* edge with a burr, not a square edge.

**Filing the edge**   File the edge of the scraper to 45° with a mill file. With the file flat on the bench, hold the scraper at a 45° angle and push it along the file length. The exact angle is not critical—I file the angle by eye.

**Honing the edge**   Hone the filed edge on an 800-grit waterstone or a fine-grit oilstone, maintaining the same angle established during the filing. Check the edge by examining the surface: Any mill marks will be visible, and you can increase or decrease the angle to remove the marks depending on where they are located. Try not to round over the edge. Run the flat face of the scraper over the stone several times to remove the burr from the file.

**Consolidating the edge**   Consolidate the edge in the same way as for a hand scraper, making a few light passes with a burnisher. Use lighter pressure than you would with a hand scraper to protect the more delicate edge.

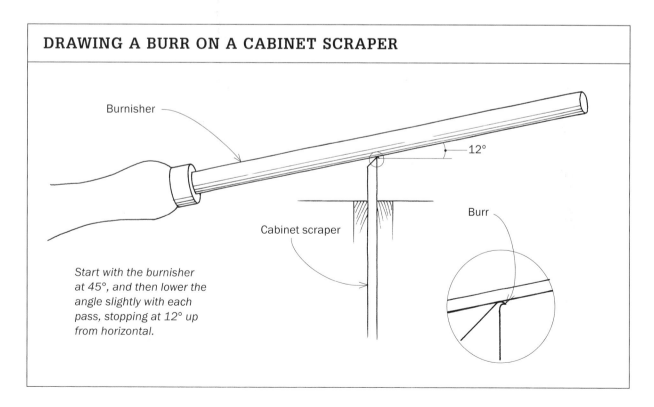

### DRAWING A BURR ON A CABINET SCRAPER

Burnisher

12°

Burr

Cabinet scraper

*Start with the burnisher at 45°, and then lower the angle slightly with each pass, stopping at 12° up from horizontal.*

***Drawing the burr***  Clamp the scraper in a vise. Holding the burnisher at the same 45° angle as the blade bevel, run the burnisher across the edge with moderate pressure. Make several more passes, gradually tilting the handle of the burnisher up and stopping at 12° up from horizontal (see the drawing on p. 25). This angle is critical because it determines the ability of the scraper with a fixed blade to cut. If the angle is less than 12°, the scraper burr will be too steep and the scraper will chatter. If the angle is too great, the scraper won't cut. Experiment to get the feel for this angle. If you have a cabinet scraper that has a tilt adjustment, you may be able to compensate for an incorrect hook angle, but try to get the angle as close as possible.

## USING SCRAPERS

As with sharpening, there are subtle differences in the way that hand scrapers and cabinet scrapers are used.

***Hand scrapers***  There are several ways to use a hand scraper. For most applications, you hold the scraper by the edges, with thumbs in the middle to flex the blade slightly away from you (see the photo below). Push the scraper away from your body, pressing downward on the scraper and adjusting the tilt of the scraper to the wood to achieve the best cutting angle. You'll feel it when you get it right. When held in this manner, the scraper will remove the

**Holding the scraper by the edges and flexing the blade out, push the scraper away from your body.**

greatest amount of material, and the wood surface will appear scalloped under a finish. If you don't want this scalloped effect, hold the scraper without flexing the blade and decrease the downward pressure. (You'll need to round the sharp corners to prevent them from digging in and marring the work.) The amount of flex can be increased to decrease the width of the shaving for scraping small areas or glue drips.

If you have a large surface (such as a tabletop) to scrape, place your hands on either side of the scraper and pull, using long sweeping motions (see the photo below). This technique does not flex the blade, so you may want to round the sharp corners slightly. Sweeping the scraper across the surface does not remove a large amount of material and leaves a near perfect surface ready for finishing.

When hand scraping, you do not have to work in any particular direction, although scraping parallel or at a slight bias to the grain leaves the best surface. Scraping across the grain is possible but results in a ragged surface. When working knots, it's best if you come in from various directions, then feather out the surface. On surfaces with pieces glued at right angles to one another, such as a bread-board top, scrape lightly at a 45° angle to avoid tearing any high ridges where the edges meet. Using a hand scraper can generate heat, which causes the metal to get quite hot. If this is a problem, wrap some electrical tape around it or use a proprietary holder.

**To scrape large surfaces, start at one end of the board and move the scraper across the surface in a sweeping motion.**

**Hand scrapers are ideal for surfacing the flat panels on frame-and-panel doors.**

***Cabinet scrapers***   To use a cabinet scraper, first slide the blade into the body from the bottom up to prevent damage to the delicate burr. The beveled edge should face toward you and the burr away from you when you're holding the tool. Place the scraper on a level wooden surface and, holding the blade down with one hand, tighten the screws that secure the blade to the body. Then lightly tighten the screw that flexes the blade in the middle. The amount that you tighten this screw determines the depth of the cut.

In use, push the cabinet scraper away from you and keep downward pressure on it so that it won't chatter. Arrange your work to allow access from all sides and secure it with bench dogs or clamps. As with the hand scraper, you can scrape in either direction of the grain or at a slight bias. To flatten large panels with a cabinet scraper, start out at a 45° angle and then reverse the angle; working this way removes high spots and levels the surface. Finish the panel by making several passes parallel to the grain.

## USES FOR SCRAPERS

Scrapers excel where other surfacing tools can't be used. Figured, rowy, and curly stock are excellent candidates for scrapers. Wood with knots should be scraped, never planed. The hand scraper gets into tight places that can't be reached with any other tool, such as the right angle formed where a leg meets an apron. Flat panels on frame-and-panel doors are another area that scrapers can surface. Cabinet scrapers are also effective in removing glue squeeze-out from edge-gluing large panels. Scrapers can be used to remove finishes, although I wouldn't recommend using them on pieces where you want to preserve the patina.

If used properly, scrapers leave an almost perfect surface, but it's best if you follow up with at least 180- to 220-grit paper before staining and finishing to remove any minor surface flaws.

## Abrasives

Preparing wood surfaces by sanding is the universally accepted way of flattening and smoothing wood. In the old days, woodworkers used bench planes and scrapers because sandpaper was costly and hard to find. Nowadays, there probably isn't a woodworker who doesn't use sandpaper to some extent. For finishing applications there are two categories of sandpaper: sandpaper used to prepare wood surfaces prior to finishing and sandpaper used between finish coats and for rubbing out finishes.

## SANDPAPER COMPONENTS

Whatever its end use, all sandpaper is comprised of the same elements—abrasive particles, a flexible backing, and glue. Abrasive particles are what remove the wood. Each particle acts like a tiny scraper, shearing off tiny pieces of wood fibers as you move the paper across the wood. The particles are either natural or synthetic minerals; the three most commonly used in finishing are garnet, aluminum oxide, and silicon carbide. Alumina zirconia and ceramic aluminum oxide are used in high-speed applications such as belt sanding. The size of the particle or grit is designated by a number. Low numbers mean larger grits, except in micron grading (see the chart on p. 30).

The abrasive particles are glued to a paper, cloth, or polyester backing, depending on the application. Paper backing is used for most wood applications and is designated by letters A through F. A is the lightest weight and F is the heaviest. The lighter weights are more flexible and as a general rule are found on finer grits. Cloth backing is used where strength is important, as on a belt sander. Polyester backing may be used where light weight and strength are important, as on a random-orbit sander.

The abrasive particles are glued to the backing with one of two types of glue. The most common is animal hide glue. Synthetic glues (phenolic or urea) are water- and heat-resistant and are used in applications such as wet sanding and high-speed machine sanding. There are two applications of glue. The first, called the make coat, anchors the mineral to the backing. The second, called the size coat, fills in the spaces between the abrasive particles.

The possible combinations of abrasive, glue, and backing are staggering, but the following are the most commonly used sanding products in wood finishing.

*Garnet* is a natural mineral that is used in hand-sanding applications. It is glued to a paper backing and sized with hide glue.

*Aluminum oxide,* a synthetic mineral, is the most widely used material for both hand and machine sanding of wood. It is used with either hide glue or synthetic resin on paper, cloth, and polyester backings. Aluminum oxide mixed with zinc stearate is sold as No-Fil or Fre-Cut papers, which do not load as quickly as standard aluminum-oxide papers and dissipate heat quicker. These papers are called stearated sandpaper and can be used on both bare wood and between coats of finish (except water-based finishes).

SANDPAPER COMPONENTS

Abrasive particles  
Glue (size coat)  
Glue (make coat)  
Backing

*Silicon carbide,* a synthetic mineral harder than aluminum oxide, is used with water-resistant glue on paper or polyester backings in wet-sanding applications. The best use for this material is for sanding dried finish between coats and for the final wet-sanding of dried finish for rubbing out.

*Alumina zirconia* and *ceramic aluminum oxide* are synthetic materials used for belt sanders. They are glued with synthetic adhesives to cloth backings and have high heat and wear resistance.

## Abrasive-Grade Comparisons

| Grade # (grit) | Generic Name | Aught Symbol | Micron Grade |
|---|---|---|---|
| 2,000<br>1,500<br>1,200 | | | 1<br>3<br>6 |
| 1,000<br>800<br>600 | Ultra fine | | 9<br><br>12 |
| 500 | | | 15<br>18<br>20 |
| 400<br>360<br>320 | Super fine<br><br>Extra fine | 0000 | 22<br>30<br>35 |
| 280<br>240<br>220 | Very fine | 000 | 40 |
| 180<br>150<br>120 | Fine | 00<br><br>0 | 60<br>80<br>100 |
| 100<br>80<br>60 | Medium | 1<br><br>2 | |
| 50<br>40<br>36 | Coarse<br><br>Extra coarse | 3<br><br>4 | |

## ABRASIVE GRADING

The abrasive industry grades sandpaper by a system of grit designations. Abrasive grits are available ranging from as low as 12 up to 2,000. For woodworking applications, grits from 36 to 1,200 are the most widely used: 36 to 60 are used for shaping on machines; 80 to 150 are used either by hand or machine for stock removal to eradicate marks from machining and dimensioning; 180 to 240 are used for smoothing the wood surface; 280 to 400 are used for between-coats smoothing; and 400 to 1200 are used for polishing finishes and rubbing out.

In addition to sandpaper, there are several products useful for between-coats preparation and polishing of finishes. Steel wool is made from steel-wool fibers spun into a pad. Steel-wool pads are graded by the aught system of numbers ranging from 0000 to 4. An alternative to steel wool is a synthetic product that is made by impregnating abrasive particles within a fiber pad (known variously as "synthetic steel wool pads," "non-woven plastic abrasive pads," etc.). This product does not shred like steel wool, and because it is nonmetallic it does not build up a static charge and cling to intricate detailed areas. 3M calls their product Scotch-Brite, and Norton's product is known as Bear-Tex. Synthetic abrasive pads are usually graded according to color. Although there is no grading standardization between manufacturers, most companies produce four colors for woodworking applications: white (equivalent to 600 to 800 grit), gray (320 to 400 grit), maroon (220 to 280 grit), and green (150 to 180 grit).

For between-coats smoothing, synthetic abrasive pads are a much better product than standard steel-wool pads. For final polishing and rubbing out, both products perform well. Neither product can be used for leveling or shaping because of its "cushion" design.

## SANDING PROGRESSION

To sand efficiently, it is important to understand the sanding progression. As explained above, sandpaper is comprised of tiny angular fragments that shear off tiny pieces of wood as the sandpaper is moved across the wood. The depth of this scratch pattern is determined by the size of the abrasive particles. When you switch to a finer grit, the depth of the scratch pattern is smaller; you should continue sanding with this grit until the finer scratch pattern removes the scratches left by the previous grit. The progression of grit changes is called the sanding schedule.

There are three main considerations when sanding. First, you should begin sanding with the finest grit capable of removing the imperfections and machine marks on the wood. This sounds

# Choosing Abrasive Materials

For general stock removal and smoothing, use 80- to 220-grit papers in aluminum oxide. For machine sanding, use longer-lasting stearated paper. If you sand only by hand, you can use garnet paper but aluminum oxide is a better all-around choice.

For between-coats sanding, 240- to 400-grit stearated paper can be used dry. Use silicon-carbide wet/dry paper in 320 to 800 grits for final rubbing out and polishing. Steel wool (0000 grade) and synthetic abrasive pads (gray and maroon grade) can also be used for between-coats sanding and final polishing.

For belt sanders, I recommend the heavy-duty abrasive belts made with alumina zirconia or ceramic aluminum oxide. 3M's Regalite is one brand name. Carry these belts in 60, 80, 100, and 120 grits.

simple, but it's amazing how many people ignore it. If you've scraped or planed wood to near perfection, it's counterproductive to begin sanding with 80 grit. All this accomplishes is to put deep sanding scratches in the wood that now should be removed by 120, 180, and then 220. It's much more efficient to start with 180 and go to 220 in this situation. The opposite of this case is also true: Trying to remove circular-saw marks with 180 is inefficient; start with 80 or 100.

Second, it's inefficient to use all grits in the sanding schedule. If you start at 80, it's okay to skip up to 120, then 180, and then 240. If you start at 100, you can switch to 150, then 220. There are no hard and fast rules, other than sanding until all the scratches left by the previous grit are gone.

Third, you should remove dust (including abrasive particles broken off from the sandpaper) from the wood as you sand. Dust loads up the spaces in between the abrasive particles and keeps the paper from cutting efficiently. Removing the dust extends the life of the paper and makes it easier to see what you're doing. The dust-collector attachments sold as accessories with power sanders are a big advantage in this situation. When the paper is dull and no longer cuts, throw it out and use new paper.

How fine you sand is up to you. Some people I know regularly sand up to 400 grit and swear they can see a difference between this grit and 240. As an experiment, I sanded a 4-ft.-long curly-maple tabletop to 120 grit. Then I divided the top into six sections and resanded the other five areas to 180, 240, 320, 400, and finally 600. I cut the top lengthwise and applied three coats of lacquer to one board and three coats of linseed oil to the other. After drying, the results were as follows: On the oil-finished board, there was a subtle sheen difference between the 180 and 600. The 180 and 240 had a lower gloss, more matte appearance, while the 320 and 600 were slightly shinier; the difference was not apparent unless viewed in the correct light. After several weeks, the differences were less apparent, even when viewed in critical light. There was little difference between the different sanded areas of the lacquer-finished board.

The results were what I expected. Finishes that form a film eventually fill in and disguise the sanding scratches and surface texture (if any) from sanding. So sanding beyond 180 or 220 isn't necessary. Oil or any penetrating finish may telegraph a slight surface-texture difference from sanding, so how high you sand is a matter of preference. Since most oil finishes are favored for their matte, natural look, I never go above 240. To go higher is a lot of extra work for a subtle luster difference that doesn't last. While a

600-grit surface may appear shiny with an oil finish on it initially, the surface of the wood gradually oxidizes to a duller appearance. There's little finish to protect it.

**HAND SANDING**

Hand sanding is regarded as the most tedious way to sand wood, but it goes more quickly if done correctly. As explained previously, start with the coarsest grit necessary to remove the irregularities and defects from the surface.

Take a sheet of sandpaper and tear it into four pieces. Use the sharp edge of a table or bench to get a clean tear. Using a cork block or a cork-faced piece of wood, wrap the sandpaper around it, holding the edges with your thumb and fingers. Always sand with the grain of the wood. Apply moderate pressure and try to keep pressure consistent throughout the stroke. Keep the block in as straight a line as possible and periodically blow the dust off the wood and the paper as it loads up. Vacuum the surface and look at the surface with backlighting to see if there are any areas that you've missed. There should be a consistent scratch pattern across the entire surface. If there's a slight hollow or machine mark, it will show up as a change in surface luster. Don't sand too hard or too long in that area to remove it; otherwise, it will show up under the finish later as a depression. Work a little of the area and then feather it out toward the rest of the surface. One more pass will blend it in.

When hand sanding, it's more efficient to make as small a grit jump as you can (say, from 120 to 150 rather than from 120 to 240). Although working this way uses more paper, once the surface is cleared of defects with the coarse grit, two passes with the next grit are all that are needed before switching.

Using a backing block on complex and curved surfaces will destroy detail, so back the paper with your palm instead. Make a cut on the short side of the paper halfway up the long side, and then fold the paper as shown in the drawing. This method of folding ensures that one abrasive surface doesn't rub against another.

**MACHINE SANDING**

Some of the best new woodworking products to come out in the past ten years have been power sanding tools and accessories. Detail/profile sanders, random-orbit sanders, and dust-collection systems were previously unavailable to the general woodworking public or prohibitively expensive. New, faster-cutting and longer-wearing abrasives are available for belt sanders and other power sanders. There are four power sanders that do an excellent job of surface preparation: belt sanders, oscillating pad sanders, random-

## FOLDING A SHEET OF SANDPAPER

*1. Make a cut halfway up on the short side.*

*2. Fold bottom-right quarter up.*

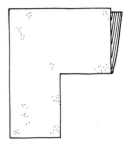

*3. Fold top-right side under.*

*4. Fold bottom half up.*

Power sanding tools include (clockwise from top left) an oscillating pad sander, random-orbit sanders (shown in right-angle and in-line models), and a profile sander.

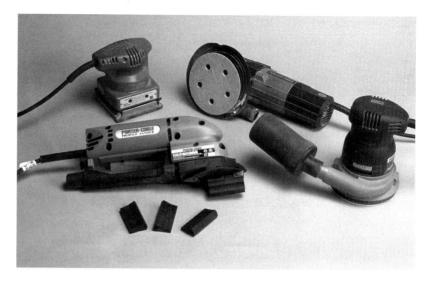

Belt sanders are available in small-belt (left) and large-belt designs (right).

orbit sanders, and detail/profile sanders. While you don't need to own all four, each one has advantages that make it particularly suited to specific tasks in surface preparation.

***Belt sanders*** The belt sander has a nasty reputation for destroying more projects than any other sanding tool, but when used correctly, this tool is indispensable. For flattening and removal of machine marks the belt sander has no equal, and for certain shaping tasks it is more versatile than a stationary sander. Belt sanders are the most aggressive portable sanding tool and the most difficult to master. They come in various sizes and weights. Large belt (4 in. x 24 in.) sanders are heavy and are best suited for flattening and heavy stock removal. Their weight is an asset when flattening large panels because it keeps the platen flat on the work. Smaller (3 in. x 21 in.)

designs are lighter weight, so freehand shaping and sanding are possible. Belt sanders can be used right up to finish grits, depending on your skill, but I prefer to switch to a random-orbit sander or pad sander because these tools are easier to control.

**Oscillating pad sanders**   Oscillating pad sanders have been around a long time and are available in several sizes. They consist of a vibrating pad that produces small, curlicue-type scratches in a repeating pattern. They are easy to control but should not be used with grits under 100. The repetitive, cross-grain scratch pattern left by coarse grits is very noticeable and hard to remove completely with the next grit.

**Random-orbit sanders**   Random-orbit sanders are relative newcomers to the general woodworking public (although air-powered commercial versions of these sanders have been around for a long time). These sanders combine two separate sanding motions—orbital and rotary. The net effect is that the two motions produce scratches that cancel each other out. The main advantage of random-orbit sanders is that you can use them for aggressive stock removal and finish sanding, something that you can't do with belt and orbital sanders.

There are two styles of random-orbit sanders—right angle and in-line. Right-angle sanders have the motor mounted at a right angle to the drive shaft. These sanders usually incorporate a more powerful motor, so aggressive stock removal is possible. In-line sanders have the motor mounted in line with the drive shaft, directly over the pad. They vary in power from small, palm-grip

Random-orbit sanders equipped with through-the-pad dust extraction are very efficient at removing dust as you sand. This vacuum is "tool triggered" (designed to operate as soon as the tool is turned on).

# Choosing a Sander

The best all-around sander is a right-angle random-orbit sander. This tool is aggressive enough for efficient stock removal and easy to control for final smoothing. Most right-angle random-orbit sanders have excellent dust removal systems. The disadvantages are that these sanders don't work on edges or in tight corners.

Belt sanders are the best for shaping, flattening, and rough stock removal, but they take practice to master. Oscillating pad sanders work better on edges and can get into corners better than belt or random-orbit sanders. Detail/profile sanders are great for cleaning up molded edges and other profiles and for getting into tight corners.

styles for light finish sanding to larger-motor designs that rival the right-angle models in power and performance.

The best feature of almost all random-orbit sanders is that they have provisions for dust collection. The most efficient collection is done through the pad itself, which has holes punched in it so that dust is vacuumed as you sand (see the photo on p. 35). A less efficient design incorporates a bag attached to the sander via an outlet port; to increase dust-collection capability, you can usually hook up the outlet port to a portable shop vacuum system with an adapter or accessory kit supplied by the manufacturer.

Sanding discs attach to the pads either by a pressure-sensitive adhesive (PSA) or by hook and loop. PSA discs are less expensive but, once removed from the pad, are hard to reattach. Hook-and-loop discs can be taken off and reattached as many times as necessary. For continuous production sanding applications, PSA is best. If you switch grits frequently, I recommend the hook-and-loop type. Most manufacturers have conversion pads or kits to convert from one system to the other.

***Detail/profile sanders*** These sanders are the most recent addition to machine sanders. Detail sanders are oscillating triangular-shaped pads that can sand in tight corners, such as inside a drawer. Profile sanders use an in-line back and forth motion for sanding profiles and complex moldings. Although these machines solve some tricky problems, proper surface preparation before assembly and use of sharp cutting bits limit their usefulness in finishing new work. They are much more useful in refinishing older furniture that can't be disassembled.

## USING MACHINE SANDERS

Using a power sander is the most efficient method of surface preparation, but incorrect technique can quickly ruin a project. While some machines can cause more damage than others, the general technique for using them is the same. The cross-hatching technique described on p. 37 accomplishes two goals, flattening the stock and smoothing it. It can be done with a belt sander followed by a random-orbit sander, or with the random-orbit sander alone.

Most problems with power sanders are caused by not holding the stock securely. A cabinetmaker's bench with dogs is by far the best method for holding stock, but if you don't have one, any large, flat surface can be used with special clamps or wedges (see the photo on the facing page). Avoid using C-clamps, since they get in the way and can snag power cords. The bench or table should be at a comfortable height and allow easy access from as many sides as possible.

It's important to hold the stock securely when using a machine sander. Here, "back-to-back" style clamps are used to hold a panel for belt sanding.

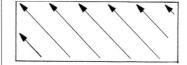
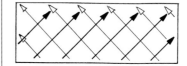
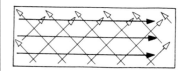
***Flattening panels with belt sanders***   Start by removing the glue from both sides of the panel. I use a cabinet scraper for this task. Then lay the panel on the bench with the good side down. Flatten the back first before beginning work on the side that will show. Start with as low a grit in the belt sander as you feel comfortable with. I routinely start with 60, then switch to 80, then 120. You can start with any grit you like; just remember that high grits take more time to accomplish the operation. I prefer to flatten with the larger, 4-in. by 24-in. sanders, but the technique will work with any sander.

Holding the sander on the panel at 45°, start the machine. (If you have a variable-speed belt sander, start with the speed at the low setting to reduce the high initial torque that can mar the panel.) Move the machine across the panel, maintaining the 45° angle. Make several passes at this angle. Change to the opposite 45° angle and repeat the operation. This cross-hatching operation knocks down high spots and levels the surface. Keep changing angles back and forth until a consistent pattern of scratches appears. Then sand with the grain until all the cross-grain scratches are removed. If the scratches are hard to see, wipe naphtha on the wood to highlight them. The back of the panel should now rest flat when placed on a level surface. If it doesn't, repeat the above operation. Then repeat the cross-hatching operation on the show side. When you have removed all the cross-grain scratches after sanding with the grain, switch to the higher grits. Using a belt sander above 120 grit to

# Special Situations

Surface preparation sometimes demands that several techniques be used together. Many times I start with a plane, switch to a scraper, and finish with fine sandpaper. Sometimes, none of these tools are appropriate for the job, and special tools or adapters for abrasives are needed. The following are common situations.

**Inside curves** These are best handled by drum sanders mounted in a drill press. The size of the drum is dictated by the degree of the curve. If you don't have a drill press, you can use a #49 or #50 Nicholson patternmaker's rasp to remove bandsaw marks. Follow the rasp with a fine file or sandpaper. For fretwork, use small detail files.

**Outside curves** These can be handled with a rasp and files, or with a pad sander. If you use a random-orbit sander, use only a hook-and-loop pad to keep the paper from flying off.

**Turned legs** Sand these while they're still on the lathe.

**Cabriole legs** Gentle curves can be smoothed with a pattern-maker's rasp, followed by filing and hand sanding.

**Complex moldings** Use a profile sander; wrapping sand-paper around dowels of various diameters works in a pinch.

**Rounded/curved forms** Use a random-orbit sander with a soft pad or sand by hand without a backing block.

**Small square spindles** The block plane works the best and the fastest, followed by light sanding. If the wood is prone to tearout, use a pad sander with a hook-and-loop pad.

**Frame-and-panel doors** Sand the panel up to the final grit, and then glue it in the door. Finish-sand the frame with a random-orbit sander.

**Tambour doors** In-line profile sanders work best.

**Carvings** Don't sand hand-carved elements—sanding will destroy the detail.

finish-sand is difficult, so I usually switch to a random-orbit sander with 120 grit at this point.

Problems occur with belt sanders if you use the incorrect stance. Stand so that it's comfortable to keep the sander's platen flat on the surface. Try not to extend the sander too far ahead of you since it can easily tip. If you have a large panel to sand, drape the cord around your neck loosely and walk the sander along the panel. Make sure that there's nothing on the bench or floor that can snag the cord. Although it's tempting to hook up a vacuum source to the belt sander, I find that it gets in the way and makes the sander hard to control.

***Flattening panels with a random-orbit sander*** The belt sander is the best tool to use for flattening, but it can be difficult to control. If you prefer, you can use the same technique with a random-orbit sander. The nice thing about this sander is that you can use it all the way from initial leveling to final smoothing. Problems occur with the random-orbit sander if you move it too fast, so try not to hurry. The machine is most effective when it remains on the surface long enough to produce scratches that cancel each other out. If you move the sander so that it covers 12 in. in 5 seconds, that's fast enough.

**Wiping the surface with naphtha helps highlight any dents.**

## Checking Surface Preparation

Before you begin finishing, always check the stock for any areas that you may have missed. Wiping the surface with naphtha or mineral spirits highlights any problem areas, such as glue drips and dents, which you should correct before moving on to staining and finishing.

Glue drips show up as light spots under a stain or finish and have to be removed. The best tool for removing glue drips is a hand scraper, particularly if the drip is in a right-angle joint. Follow the scraper with the last grit sandpaper in your sanding schedule. If it requires more than several light scrapes to remove the glue, be sure to feather the area you worked into the rest of the piece.

Steam dents out with distilled water, using a rag and an old soldering pencil with the tip removed or a clothes iron. As long as there isn't any wood missing, the fibers will swell and come level

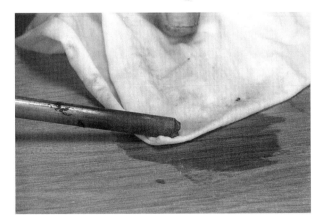

**Steam a dent with an old soldering pencil (with the tip removed) and a wet rag.**

**The small dark spot left after steaming can be removed with light sanding.**

with the rest of the surface. There may be a small dark spot left, which can be removed with the last grit in your sanding schedule.

Methods for filling gouges vary depending on the type of finish used. For woods that are left unstained, mix some of the sawdust from sanding with 5-minute epoxy for a patch that matches the surrounding wood. For woods that will be stained, commercial water-based putties work well. Apply the putty before the last grit in the sanding schedule. When the putty is dry, sand the surface flush with your last grit, and then apply the stain. Since the putty usually stains a different color from the surrounding wood, you'll have to experiment to get the right color after the stain is applied. The technique that works best is to leave the putty lighter, and then blend in the area after applying stain and a sealer coat by mixing artist pigments with shellac.

After filling a gouge with wood putty, blend the putty to the right color using dry pigments mixed with shellac.

To stabilize a large knot, glue in slivers of wood from the same board or species. You may have to put tape on the other side of the board to prevent epoxy from dripping through.

An alternate technique is to drill out the defect and patch it with a tapered plug drilled out from a similar board. The advantage of this technique is that the repair becomes less visible as you stain and finish it. Use a very sharp Forstner bit to drill out the defect.

Fill small hairline cracks with a squirt of cyanoacrylate glue, then immediately sand to mix with the glue while it's still wet to fill the crack. Larger cracks should be spliced in with wood from a similar board. Never use putty on cracks since it will shrink and eventually fall out.

Small pin knots on woods that receive a natural finish can be filled with gap-filling cyanoacrylate glue and then be sanded. On woods that are stained, use tinted putty or epoxy. Large knots with gaps or loose areas need to be stabilized. Cut slivers of the same species of wood and glue them in with clear 5-minute epoxy (see the photo at right on the facing page). Increasing the mix ratio to 2 parts resin to 1 part hardener results in a harder epoxy that scrapes and sands much better when cured.

# 3

# Coloring the Wood and Filling the Grain

Whether wood should be stained probably generates more debate among woodworkers than whether pins or tails should be cut first on dovetails. Some argue that you should leave wood alone since it changes color naturally over time. Others contend that staining wood can enhance its natural beauty and create an aged, antique look without having to wait years for the natural process. Also, many woods look better when stained (particularly drab and monotonous woods). There are arguments for both sides, but they tend to delve into philosophical and artistic differences that are well beyond the scope of this book. While staining is an optional aesthetic choice when finishing a new project, it's often a necessity if you restore or refinish furniture.

Understanding the subject of staining can be intimidating for the woodworker because there is such a wide variety of staining materials available, with distinct usage and handling differences. Much of the confusion generated over the years is from terminology, so let's start with a basic definition. In this country, the coatings industry (the people who make finishing products) defines a *stain* as a product that imparts a color change to the surface of wood without obscuring the substrate. This last part is important, because it is what distinguishes a stain from a paint, whose function is precisely the opposite. Paints are formulated to cover up or obscure the substrate.

The materials used to color wood
are available in different colorant
types and formulations. Shown here
are the two most popular classes:
pigmented stains and dye stains.

Stains are further classified as pigment-type, dye-type, and
chemical-type. All three types produce a color change in wood,
but each imparts a color change differently.

## Pigmented Stains

Pigmented stains are comprised of three components: pigment,
carrier, and binder. By changing either the carrier or the binder,
different formulations for different applications are possible.

### PIGMENT

Pigmented stains use dry pigment as the colorant. Pigment is a
colored powder that is insoluble in the carrier/binder that it is
applied in. Pigment powder can be either a natural product or
man-made.

The majority of the natural pigments used in wood stains are
mined from the earth and are called earth colors and iron oxides.
Earth colors (i.e., the siennas, ochres, and umbers) are an older
designation still used by artists. Earth pigments are used extensively
in wood stains because they duplicate natural wood colors, ranging
from light yellows to reddish-oranges and deep, rich browns. They
are naturally transparent because they have a high silica content,
and are muted in terms of brightness—qualities naturally desirable
in wood stains. Iron oxides are generally more opaque because they
contain much less silica.

Man-made pigments are used where bright and vivid colors are
required. Blues, bright yellows, reds, and whites are always man-
made pigments. Some of the iron oxides are also man-made.

Unfortunately, there's no way to tell which pigments are used in any particular wood stain because manufacturers do not use the above color designations. Instead, a burnt sienna pigment could be called cherry, and burnt umber could be called walnut. Usually, different pigments are intermixed to achieve various colors like antique cherry or dark Jacobean oak. Because these are names chosen by the manufacturer and they are based on a subjective interpretation of what wood color the pigment resembles, there is no consistency between manufacturers. One company's light walnut might be the same as another's golden oak.

## CARRIER

You can't just take a handful of dry pigment, spread it over a piece of wood, and expect it to color the wood. A liquid is necessary to apply the dry powder evenly over the surface of the wood. This liquid, which is called the carrier, is different depending on the class of stain. Oil-based stains use mineral spirits for the carrier, water-based stains use water, and lacquer-based stains use lacquer thinner. Manufacturers usually list the carrier, but if they don't, look for the solvent that they recommend to thin or clean up the stain with. Carriers never become part of the dried stain because they evaporate.

The oak board on the left telegraphs its prominent pore structure with a pigment stain. The birch panel on the right has a more even distribution of pores, so the stain takes more evenly.

## BINDER

If stains were made only of pigment and carrier, when the carrier evaporated there would still be dry powder lying on the wood, which you could easily blow off or remove when you wiped or brushed a finish over it. A substance is required to provide adhesion of the particles to the wood surface and to each other. This is the job of the binder, which must be compatible with the carrier used. There are dozens of binders suitable for stain formulations, but the oldest and traditional binder is a drying oil like linseed or tung oil. These stains, known as oil-based stains, cure slowly, so manufacturers sometimes add a small amount of varnish resin and metallic driers to speed up the dry time. Water-based stains use an emulsified oil or acrylic/urethane binder similar to the resins used in water-based lacquers. Lacquer-based wood stains use small amounts of solvent lacquer.

By changing the carrier or binder, manufacturers are able to offer stains in fast-dry formulations (lacquer, ester gum) or in low-flammable and less hazardous formulations (water-based). Oil-based formulations are the most common and can be used under most finishes, except some water-based lacquers. Lacquer-based and water-based formulations work under any finish, although applying some finishes over a lacquer-based stain may redissolve the binder and pick up color from the stain. Some manufacturers add a gelling agent to a standard oil formulation. These stains are easier to handle and don't drip on vertical areas. They also solve some tricky staining problems such as splotching (see pp. 60-61). For brushing and wiping finishes, certain pigmented-stain/finish combinations work better than others, which I'll explain later (see p. 62).

## HOW PIGMENT STAINS WOOD

Pigment particles are small enough to be seen with the naked eye or under low magnification (10x). When applied over the surface of wood and then wiped, the particles lodge in pores, sanding scratches, and any cavities larger than the size of the pigment particle—including defects. Woods with prominent pores like oak and ash telegraph their pore structure with pigmented stains. Even-textured woods like birch accept stain evenly because of the even distribution of the pores (see the photo on the facing page). Very dense woods like maple do not readily accept stain when sanded to 240 grit because there are hardly any crevices for the pigment to lodge in. However, when sanded to 100 grit, maple takes pigment in the sanding scratches (see the photo at right).

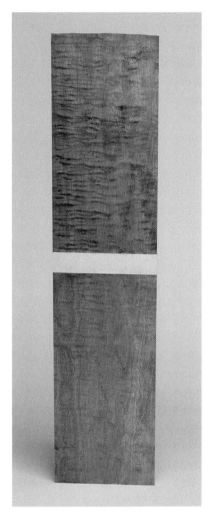

**The top half of this maple board (sanded to 100 grit) stained darker than the bottom half (sanded to 240 grit) because there were more cavities for the stain to lodge in.**

## APPLYING PIGMENTED STAINS

Pigmented stains are popular because they are easy to apply. The stain is brushed or wiped on evenly, and the excess is wiped off while the stain is still wet. The amount of time you have to wipe off the stain depends on the evaporating rate of the carrier and the type of binder. Quick-drying lacquer stains dry the quickest, followed by water-based, and then oil and oil/varnish blends.

Pigmented stains can obscure the wood grain if they're not wiped off completely. While you can manipulate the intensity of color by varying the amount of stain you leave on the surface, the best effects are achieved by wiping off the excess. To make sure that the final color is exactly what you want, experiment on cutoffs sanded to the same grit as your project. A stain on one wood may appear slightly different on another—particularly if the pore structure is different. You can lighten the stain by wiping the surface with the carrier for the stain before it dries, or adjust the color slightly by applying a different or darker-color stain before the first one dries. Oil-based and water-based stains can't be corrected when cured, except by stripping or sanding off the stain.

Certain stains will redissolve when the finish top coats are applied by brush or by pad. Generally, these are the quick-dry stains that have little or no binder. Lacquer will redissolve lacquer stains and pick it up off the wood. Stains that have very little binder come off easily when brushed or padded. Water-based finishes will redissolve water-based stains, although the problem is not as severe as with lacquer. Oil-based stains, when fully dry, do not redissolve under any finish so these are the best choice when brushing or wiping. Sealing water-based and lacquer stains by lightly flowing on a wash coat of dilute shellac remedies the problem of redissolving, but you may want to switch to a dye stain, as explained below.

# Dye Stains

The chemistry of dye stains is much more complex than that of pigment-based stains, but the most immediate difference is a physical one. Pigmented stains hold colored particles (pigment) in suspension in the carrier/binder mix. Dyes are colored chemical compounds that are dissolved in a solvent carrier. Whereas pigmented stains are made up of pigment, carrier, and binder, dye stains are comprised of only dye and carrier.

**Pigment-based stains (left) usually hold the coloring matter in suspension; the pigment settles to the bottom. Dye stains (right) are true solutions; the coloring matter never settles out.**

## CHEMICAL COMPOSITION

Dye stains were originally derived from fruits, berries, roots, and other natural materials. The dye was extracted by boiling these materials in water. These dyes were not very "lightfast" (resistant to fading in light). Methods were devised to overcome this problem by complex processes that rendered the dye less prone to fading, but it wasn't until the latter part of the 19th century that chemists were able to synthesize dyes that eventually replaced the natural dyes.

When dyes were first synthesized chemically in 1856, the principal starting ingredient was aniline, a liquid chemical that, at the time, was a by-product of the burning of coal. The term *aniline dyes* was coined at that time to distinguish these dyes from the older natural dyes like indigo and logwood. The term aniline has stuck, and most wood, textile, and leather dyes are sold today as aniline dyes, even though aniline may not be used in the synthesis of the dye.

Dyes can be put into solution with a wide variety of solvents, depending on the dye. The most common carriers are water, alcohol, and oil (hydrocarbons like mineral spirits, naphtha, and toluene). Every dye has a solvent that it dissolves best in, and this is listed by the manufacturer as the solvent for that dye.

Dyes for wood are sold in two forms, either as a dry powder or premixed. Powdered dyes need to be dissolved in the appropriate solvent by the user. Premixed dyes are dissolved into solvent or a blend of solvents by the manufacturer and sold to finishers ready-to-use.

## POWDERED DYES

Powdered dyes are generally grouped into three categories: water-soluble, alcohol-soluble, and oil-soluble. Each dye group has general features and handling characteristics, although there are exceptions within each group.

***Water-soluble dyes***   Water-soluble dyes have the best all-around characteristics of all the dye powders. They are economical and easy to use, penetrate the best, and have good-to-excellent lightfastness. The choice of colors is quite extensive, and many suppliers offer a dazzling array of wood tones, primary colors, and secondary colors. Their one drawback is that they raise the grain of the wood.

***Alcohol-soluble dyes***   Alcohol-soluble dyes do not raise the grain of the wood. Depending on the dye groups that the manufacturer uses, they can have excellent or poor lightfastness. Some are superior to the water-soluble dyes in this respect. Fortunately, most manufacturers tell you whether or not their alcohol dyes are light-fast. You can expect to pay more for the light-stable dyes than for the fugitive (nonlightfast) ones.

**Alcohol-soluble dyes that are lightfast (left) retain their color after exposure to ambient light, whereas alcohol-soluble dyes that are nonlightfast (right) fade quickly.**

Most alcohol-soluble dyes produce crisp, vivid colors. Methanol or ethanol (denatured alcohol) works as a solvent for the dyes for most purposes, but on porous-textured woods like ash and mahogany, pore bleeding may result because the alcohol dries too fast. The problem is similar to pore bleeding of oil finishes (see p. 109). The remedy for this problem is to add a glycol-ether retarder for dyes (manufacturers provide these as additives). Solvent-lacquer retarders can also be used.

***Oil-soluble dyes*** At one time, oil-soluble dyes were the workhorse of the furniture industry, primarily because they did not raise the grain. However, they are rarely used today because of two annoying characteristics: They have a tendency to bleed into finish top coats, and they lack the brightness and crispness of water- and alcohol-soluble dyes. On the positive side, they are extremely easy to use. Oil-soluble dyes penetrate quickly, and they dry slowly enough (depending on the carrier) to give you sufficient time to wipe off the excess. They dissolve in a wide variety of solvents, including turpentine, mineral spirits, kerosene, naphtha, toluene, and lacquer thinner.

## PREMIXED DYES

The largest class of premixed dyes is known as NGR (non-grain-raising) dye stains. Although formulations vary, most manufacturers use a class of light-stable, water-soluble dyes known as metallized-acid dyes. This group of dyes dissolves best in water but also has moderate solubility in methanol and glycol-ether solvents. These dye stains are manufactured by mixing the dry powder with a glycol ether and then adding methanol; the solution is strained to remove undissolved dye. This type of dye gives the user all the benefits of using a water-soluble dye, but without the grain raising. The downside is that the solvent blend is flammable and toxic. The methanol can be replaced by water, and these formulations are sold as premixed, water-based dye stains. The elimination of methanol makes the product less polluting and nonflammable.

## HOW DYES STAIN WOOD

When put into the correct solvent, the dye ionizes, or breaks down, into extremely small, electrically charged particles, some of which carry the color. These particles are so small that a powerful microscope is needed to see them; for comparison purposes, they are about 1,000 times smaller than the smallest pigment particle. This small size is what allows the coloring particles to penetrate deep into the wood fibers and evenly color very dense woods like hard maple from the brightest of yellows to the blackest of blacks.

These two pine legs were colored with a dye stain (left) and a pigmented stain (right). The dye stain colors more evenly because it penetrates all areas of the wood evenly, while the pigmented stain exaggerates grain differences.

On a turned leg, this feature shows as even coloration, even though the wood surface changes from flat grain to end grain (see the photo at left). Dye stains are characterized as transparent, because the particles are so small that they absorb and transmit light as it strikes the surface of the wood. (Larger pigment particles absorb and reflect light back, which makes them look opaque.) This transparency allows the grain and subtle nuances to show through even if the color of the dye is very dark.

Dye stains do not have a binder like pigmented stains. The ionized particles become attached to the wood fiber by molecular forces. In a sense, they are bound to the wood fiber with an electronic "binder." Not only do dye stains penetrate deeply, but they also stay put, and removal can be accomplished only with strong bleach or by sanding.

### APPLYING DYE STAINS

Dye stains are applied differently than pigmented stains. The ease with which a dye stain can be applied by hand depends on the carrier. Let's look at water-soluble dyes first.

***Water-soluble dyes***  Water-soluble dyes should be dissolved in hot water according to the manufacturer's instructions; they are normally ready to use by the time the solution has cooled to room temperature. Some manufacturers (for example, Behlen and Mohawk) use both water- and alcohol-soluble dyes in the powder, so you need to mix in methanol first before adding water. Most dye stains do not need to be strained, although it's a good idea to strain the dye if you use it right after mixing to prevent large undissolved dye particles from streaking the wood.

Since water raises the grain, it's necessary to preraise the grain. I use distilled water and sponge the wood liberally. An alternate method is to use a very dilute solution of the dye. After the wood is dry, sand with the last grit in your sanding schedule. Flood the surface with dye from a rag, brush, or sponge, and work it quickly to cover the surface. Wet the entire surface with dye until it's uniformly saturated, and then let the dye sit until dry. There's no need to blot up excess dye, as you would with a pigmented stain. On chairs and other complex items, this feature of water dyes is a blessing. On frame-and-panel doors or other complex surfaces, use a small brush or a used synthetic abrasive pad (see p. 31) to work the dye into crevices and corners.

The color of the wood when wet with dye is not necessarily the same as the color when it is finished. To get a good idea of whether the intensity and shade are correct, allow the dye to dry completely,

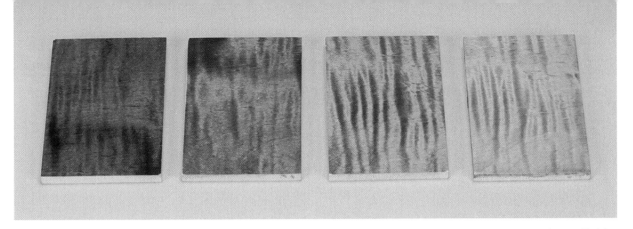

Water-soluble dyes can be applied in stronger or weaker concentrations to achieve different intensities.

and then wipe it with mineral spirits or naphtha. However, dyes shift in shade depending on the finish applied, so the only way to be truly accurate is to practice on some samples (see the photo above) and finish them with several coats of the finish you'll be using. To make a dye stain stronger, add more dye to the solution; to make a dye stain weaker, add more water. To lighten up a surface that's already dyed, apply clean water with a clean rag before the dye is fully dry. You can remove quite a bit of color, though never all of it.

On wood with very pronounced pores like oak and ash, you may notice that the pores do not accept the dye stain and remain uncolored. It is the reverse effect of pigmented stains. There are a couple of ways to deal with this. One is to use a colored paste-wood filler to fill and color the pores at the same time (see p. 69). The other is to color the pores with a pigmented glaze or stain after sealing the dye with finish (see p. 64).

**Alcohol-soluble dyes, NGR dyes**   I don't recommend using alcohol-soluble dyes unless they are reasonably lightfast. Some powdered alcohol dyes are so poor in lightfastness that they fade significantly after one or two weeks' exposure to ambient light.

Alcohol-soluble dyes are dissolved in either methanol or ethanol (denatured alcohol). I recommend using ethanol because it is far less toxic and less hazardous than methanol. Some of these dyes also dissolve in ketones (acetone, methyl ethyl ketone), glycol ethers, and aromatic hydrocarbons like toluene. After dissolving the dry dye powder, it's a good idea to strain the solution because some alcohol-soluble dyes do not dissolve completely.

When applying alcohol-soluble dyes, the choice of solvent is critical. Straight alcohol evaporates very quickly, causing lap marks. On porous and figured woods, you may experience bleeding of still wet dye back up and around the pores, making dark circles.

## COLOR WHEEL

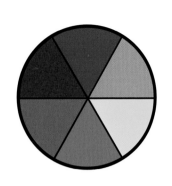

A color wheel organizes primary and secondary colors and serves as a visual tool for understanding color theory.

I suggest that you always add a retarder to the alcohol. The retarder slows down the overall drying time, making the dye easier to apply, and eliminates bleeding. Alcohol-dye retarder is available from most suppliers. Lacquer retarder also works.

Alcohol-soluble dyes and NGR dyes are applied in the same way. You can use a brush on small to mid-sized items, but on large surfaces like tabletops I find that it's easier and quicker to apply the dye with a solvent-dampened rag or sponge. Rather than flooding on the dye, it's better to work with less dye to control the dye distribution. Dab the rag or sponge in a shallow pan filled with dye and start wiping it on with the grain of the wood. If you work quickly enough and apply the dye evenly, you can apply the dye in any direction, but until you get the hang of this technique, work with the grain. Build up to the color intensity you want by applying more dye gradually. If you see a drip, try to fix it right away. Because the dye evaporates quickly, drip marks and other mistakes can be hard to blend in later when the dye is dry.

You can lighten the color by applying dye solvent with a rag. You can darken the color by applying more dye, but only to a point.

***Oil-soluble dyes*** Oil dyes dissolved in fast-drying solvents like lacquer thinner, toluene, or naphtha can be applied in the same way as alcohol-soluble and NGR dyes. When using slower-drying solvents like turpentine and mineral spirits, the dyes can be flooded on the surface and then the excess can be wiped off. Oil-soluble dyes lack the clarity and lightfastness of the water-soluble and lightfast alcohol dyes, so I discourage their use.

### CHANGING THE COLOR OF THE DYE

Because dye stains penetrate deeply and are transparent, you see the color of the dye *and* the natural color of the wood on dyed wood surfaces. So if you apply a dye to the wood and it's not quite the color you want, you can change the color (sometimes dramatically) by wiping different-colored dyes right over the dye you applied. Because dye stains have no binder, you can color-correct the dye when it's still wet or when it's fully dry.

To understand how to change the color of a dye, you need to know a little color theory. Look at the color wheel at left. Red, yellow, and blue are the primary colors. Mixing red and yellow produces orange. (Note that orange is between red and yellow on the color wheel.) Mix blue and yellow to get green (green is between blue and yellow). Mix red and blue to produce purple (purple is between blue and red). Orange, green, and purple are called secondary colors. If you apply a yellow dye to a board and then apply red over it, the dye mixes on the board to produce an overall effect of orange (see the photos below). If you then apply a dilute blue dye over the orange, you'll get an overall effect of a reddish brown. Brown is a mixture of various amounts of red, yellow, and blue.

Now here's where it gets tricky. Say the color is too red. Look on the color wheel for red and find the color opposite it. It's green. If you add a dilute green dye to the board, it will neutralize the red without darkening the color too much. Colors opposite each other on the color wheel are called complementary colors. If a color is too orange, add the complement—blue. If a color is too purple, add yellow. To darken a color, add black. By adding another color over another dye, you could theoretically continue to change the color ad infinitum, but only up to a certain point. Wood can hold only so

## Changing the Color of a Dye

1. Applying yellow dye to a board.

2. Applying red dye over yellow produces orange.

3. Applying blue dye over orange produces brown.

4. Applying a green dye over a reddish brown kills the red without darkening the color too much.

# Problem Solving with Dye Stains

Dye stains can be used to solve many finishing problems. Three of the most common uses are to blend sapwood into heartwood color, to make figure in figured woods like curly maple and cherry stand out, and to warm cool woods like poplar and kiln-dried walnut. Spectacular creative effects like sunbursts are also possible.

cloth around your finger and dab it into the dye stain. Wipe the dye on in long quick strokes on the sapwood. If the color is too dark, stop and immediately wipe the dye with alcohol to lighten it. Wipe some more mineral spirits over the board to see if you got close enough; chances are the color will still be off.

Keep wiping dilute dye on the sapwood, adding red, yellow, or green to adjust the color as necessary. Build the color in layers until it matches the heartwood. Remember, a perfect match at this point isn't necessary. As you build up finish, the two areas will blend together. If the distinction is still off as you

## Blending

You can blend sapwood into heartwood with water-soluble dye stains, but I prefer to use alcohol-soluble or NGR dyes because they dry much more quickly and do not raise the grain. Begin by sanding the wood to the desired grit, and then wipe with mineral spirits to approximate the color of the heartwood when finished. Pick a dye that matches the lightest background color of the heart-wood. Pour some of the mixed dye in a small, shallow can like a tuna can. Wrap some clean cotton

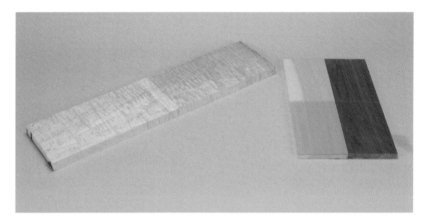

Applying a dilute amber-colored dye stain accentuates the top half of the curly-maple board on the left, and warms up the cool tones of poplar and kiln-dried walnut (bottom right). The dye stain was also used to blend sapwood into heartwood on the poplar side.

much dye, and eventually the wood surface becomes "overloaded" and will show the color of the last dye on the surface.

When working with bold primary colors, it's fairly easy to put color theory into practice. Unfortunately, wood-tone colors are harder to color-correct because they are mixtures of various amounts of red, blue, and yellow. To apply color theory to wood-tone shades, you'll have to look for the dominant primary color. If this is unfamiliar territory, it sometimes helps to think of colors in apply clear top coats, then correct the color with glazing (see p. 64) or more applications of dilute dye mixed with shellac.

## Enhancing figure

Figured woods sometimes need a little "kick" to bring out the figure, surface shimmer, and luster. Using extremely dilute solutions of an amber-brown dye will enhance figured areas like curl, bird's-eye, and swirl area around knots. In this instance, dilute means approximately eight times the normal solution, although you'll need to experiment.

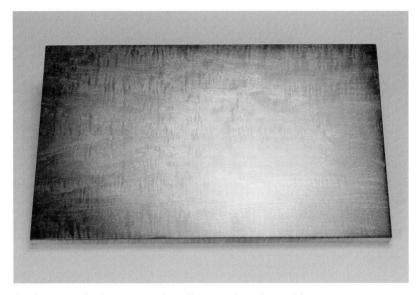

Sunbursts and other spectacular effects are best done with alcohol-soluble dye stains.

## Warming

Cool woods like poplar and kiln-dried walnut can be warmed up by applying a dilute amber-colored dye stain, as shown in the photo on the facing page. Most dye companies sell an amber or honey dye that works fine, or you can make your own by mixing 15 parts yellow, 1 part black, and 1 part red.

## Sunbursts

Dye stains also lend themselves to spectacular creative effects like shading and sunbursts (see the photo above). Alcohol-soluble dyes are better for these effects, because they are easier to manipulate by hand than water-soluble dyes. To create a sunburst or shading, work from the lightest color to the darkest, changing rags each time you change color. Blend areas of color with a clean, dry rag.

terms of warmth or coolness. A red or orange dominance is sometimes referred to as "warm" color. "Cool" colors have blue and green as the dominant colors. To cool a color, add blue or green. To warm a color, add red or orange. Yellow is the most luminous primary color. To brighten or intensify a color, add yellow. To decrease brightness, add black. To darken a color without decreasing the brightness, add brown.

## Chemical Stains: Warning

Most chemicals used as stains are poisonous and caustic—they will cause skin burns and eye damage if splashes occur. Proper handling of these products requires use of chemical gloves, an organic-vapor respirator mask rated for the appropriate chemicals, and chemical safety glasses. It is advisable to use some of the chemicals, especially ammonia, outside.

## Chemical Stains

Chemical stains predate the use of aniline dyes and were a very popular method of coloring wood until dye stains became widely available. Dozens of chemicals can be used to produce a color change in wood, but there are five that produce effects that are hard to duplicate with other coloring methods: sodium hydroxide (lye), potassium dichromate, ammonium hydroxide (ammonia), iron acetate (iron buff), and nitric acid. (These chemicals are available from Chem Lab Supplies, 1060 Ortega Way, Unit C, Placentia, CA 92670; 714-630-7902.) All produce colors that are useful in matching antique colors and colors that are difficult to achieve with pigmented stains and dye stains.

Most of these chemicals react with tannic acid, which is normally present in some woods. A third chemical is formed that is precipitated within the fibers of the wood. Chemical stains perform much like dye stains, although they require a little more experimentation to use effectively.

### SODIUM HYDROXIDE (LYE)

Sodium hydroxide reacts with tannic acid in woods like cherry, birch, mahogany, walnut, and oak to simulate the natural patina that would normally take many years to develop. Drain openers may contain sodium hydroxide as the main ingredient, but I don't recommend their use because other chemicals may be added. I use "Red Devil" household lye, which is pure lye. Dissolve 1 or more teaspoons in a quart of hot water and dilute to achieve the effect that you want. When the wood is dry, neutralize with a wash of 1 part white vinegar to 2 parts water. When dry, sand and apply finish.

**The final color of a chemical stain can be controlled by changing the concentration of the chemical (as in the lye-treated cherry board at top) or by pretreating with tannic acid (as in the left side of the potassium-dichromate-treated maple board at bottom).**

## POTASSIUM DICHROMATE

Potassium dichromate produces rich browns that cannot be duplicated with modern dyes. The chemical is dissolved in water in the ratio of 1 to 3 tablespoons to 1 qt. of water. Colors range from dark brownish-purple to medium reddish-brown. This chemical is very poisonous, so extreme care should be taken when handling and using it. The full color takes several hours to develop, so overnight drying is advised.

One of the best uses for potassium dichromate is on mahogany or cherry where light-colored inlays of maple of holly are used. The potassium dichromate darkens the tannin-containing wood and leaves the lighter-colored inlays unchanged.

## AMMONIUM HYDROXIDE (AMMONIA)

This chemical is available as a 28% aqueous ammonium-hydroxide solution, which can be applied by brush or by fuming. Ammonia fuming was a popular method of finishing oak at the turn of the century and produces a variety of colors from light honey-brown to grayish-brown. Fuming involves concentrating the fumes within an airtight compartment. Large plastic tents made with 1x2s and plastic work fine. Unless you can construct something extremely airtight, put it outdoors. Pour ammonia into several open shallow dishes and place them in the tent along with the furniture. The color effect depends on how long the wood is exposed—generally, the longer the wood is exposed the darker it gets. Ammonium hydroxide is a severe caustic and the fumes are very irritating. Make sure you wear an organic-vapor respirator mask with a cartridge rated for ammonia.

Ammonia needs to be neutralized after drying with a solution of 1 part white vinegar to 2 parts water. Always use fresh ammonia. Old solutions lose their effectiveness over several years of storage.

## IRON ACETATE (IRON BUFF)

Iron acetate is easily made by unraveling some 0000 steel wool, wetting it, and leaving it out to rust for a day or so. Shred the steel wool and soak it in 1 pt. of white vinegar for several days in an unstopped bottle (gas is produced and could explode in a stopped bottle). Decant the liquid on top and strain it through a fine-mesh strainer. Applied to walnut, mahogany, cherry, and other woods that contain tannin, iron acetate produces a rich, positive black. On woods that do not contain tannin, such as maple and pine, it creates a weathered, silver-gray. By shortening the time that the steel wool

The six sample boards were treated with, from top to bottom, lye, potassium dichromate, nitric acid, iron buff, ammonia, and no treatment. The woods are the same on each board: from left to right, pine, mahogany, maple, walnut, and white oak.

# Choosing a Stain

There are advantages and disadvantages to each of the three stain groups discussed in this chapter. Generalizations are difficult to make because woods react differently to the various stains, but the following guidelines should help steer you in the right direction.

## Pigmented stains

Pigmented stains accentuate the pores and provide contrast to the surrounding wood when wiped off. End grain stains darker. When not wiped off completely, pigmented stains can even out variations on the wood surface but will obscure figure and grain nuances. Very dense woods like maple can be hard to stain, and bright bold coloration is not possible without creating a painted effect. Pigmented stains with oil or varnish binders are best for brushing or wiping on finishes. Depending on the carrier/binder, pigmented stains can be difficult to repair or color-correct when dry. Pigmented stains based on earth colors are the most lightfast colorants to use where strong light will be present.

**Dye stains (top) color different woods more evenly, making them look similar (from left to right, the woods are maple, birch, and poplar). Pigmented stains (bottom) react to the different pore structure and surface texture, making the three woods appear very different from one another.**

## Dye stains

Dye stains provide bold, vivid coloration while letting grain and figure still show. They color wood more evenly, and end grain is less pronounced. Dye stains penetrate deeper than pigmented stains, which tend to sit on top of the wood. Dyes can be repaired easily when dry, and the color can be significantly altered. They are not as lightfast as pigments.

## Chemical stains

Chemical stains provide effects that mimic the natural patination of the wood. They are permanently attached to wood fibers and are a good choice when brushing or wiping finishes because color won't pull off with the finish. They color wood like dyes, but are not as brilliant. The big downside to chemical stains is that they are tricky to apply and are generally caustic and poisonous.

soaks in the vinegar, various shades of gray can be produced. Don't bother storing the iron-acetate solution—it starts to lose its effectiveness shortly after it is made.

## NITRIC ACID

Nitric acid produces a very convincing aged effect on maple and especially on pine. It is an extremely dangerous chemical to work with full-strength, so I recommend using a 10% to 20% solution. After applying the nitric acid, heat the wood with an electric heat gun to develop the full color effect. Then neutralize the nitric acid with a solution of baking soda dissolved in water (3 tablespoons baking soda dissolved in 1 pt. hot water). Allow at least one week drying time before finishing.

## APPLYING CHEMICAL STAINS

Chemical stains are used much like water-soluble dye stains (see pp. 50-51). Before application, preraise the grain and, when dry, resand using the last grit in your sanding schedule. Apply the chemical with a cheap, synthetic-bristle brush or sponge and always wear chemical gloves. Work quickly to saturate the surface, and then blot up the excess. In many cases the full color may take a while to develop, even after the board appears to be dry. I recommend you wait at least 24 hours before finishing.

Lye, ammonia, iron buff, and potassium dichromate all react with the tannin naturally present in certain woods. Birch, cherry, mahogany, oak, and walnut all contain tannin and react with the chemicals to produce pleasing wood tones. On woods that contain little or no tannin, you can still produce a reaction by pretreating the wood with tannic acid. Dissolve several tablespoons of tannic acid in 1 pt. of hot water, and, when the solution is cool, apply liberally to the wood. When dry, the tannic acid reacts with the chemicals (see the photo on p. 56). Sapwood does not contain tannic acid. By pretreating the sapwood with tannic acid, you can bring it in line with the color of the rest of the wood. After drying, fine-tune the color difference with alcohol-soluble dyes or NGR dyes or glazing.

Different concentrations of the chemical produce different colors. Increasing or diluting the concentration darkens or lightens the effect accordingly. Make sure to record the concentrations so you can duplicate them later.

# Controlling Stain Penetration

Many woods do not stain well, and much of the fear of staining has been caused by problems with these woods. There are four woods that are almost always subject to uneven staining, or "splotching" as it called—pine, cherry, birch, and soft maple.

The reason these woods are hard to stain lies in the structure of the wood itself. The density of the cellular structure changes in certain areas, causing more or less colorant to be absorbed into the wood. There are also natural resins present in wood, which may explain uneven penetration on woods like pine. There are two main ways to combat this problem, both based on the principle of controlling the penetration of the stain into the wood.

The first way to control penetration is to use nonpenetrating stains. Stains that are formulated with a gelled binder/carrier penetrate less overall, so the coloring is more even. Gelled pigment-based stains work very well in this situation, especially on pine (see the top photo below).

The pine board on the left has a standard pigmented stain on the left side and a gel stain on the right; the gel stain splotched less. The pine board on the right was treated with a preconditioner on the right side, and a pigmented stain was applied to both sides; the treated side splotched less.

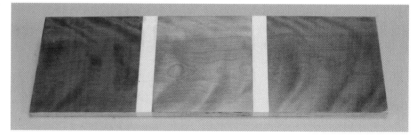

The swirly grain on this birch board causes uneven dye-stain penetration. Thinned shellac (center) and hide glue (right) were applied as a pretreatment, both resulting in less pronounced splotching than on the untreated section (left), but the shellac significantly lightened the color of the dye.

On these three resawn cherry boards traditional methods of applying gelled stains (left) and washcoating (center) failed to control splotching, but glazing (bottom right) produced acceptable results. The top half of the board at right is natural cherry.

The second way to control penetration is to apply a thinned finish to the surface of the wood to partially seal it. This technique, known as washcoating, blocks uneven absorption of the stain into the wood. The type of sealer you should use varies, depending on the type of stain you use over it. Thinned-oil finishes, which are called stain controllers or "preconditioners," are effective with oil-based pigmented stains. Thinned 1-lb. cut shellac or very dilute premixed hide glue (1 part glue to 10 parts water) can be used with water-based dyes and pigmented stains (see the bottom photo on the facing page).

Washcoating and applying gelled stains work in most cases, but because wood is not a consistent material, a technique that works for one project may be totally ineffective on another. It's important to experiment on cutoffs from the project that you're staining and to carry the finishing process to the end to predict the results accurately. For stubborn woods like cherry, it's best to get a coat of finish on the wood, and then work to the color you want the wood to be by applying glazes between coats of finish (see the photo above and pp. 62-65). You can also put color in the finish by dissolving dye in the clear finish, or use a naturally dark finishing material like some of the dark shellacs.

# Combining Dyes and Pigments

Many manufacturers recognize the difference in effects between pigments and dyes and combine both in the same can. For example, Minwax uses pigment and an oil-soluble dye in their oil-based wiping stains. These products combine the pore-coloring effect of pigment with the evenness of a dye. You can create the same effect by using dyes and pigments in separate operations. Apply a dye stain first, let it dry, and then apply a pigmented stain. The only problem with this method is that the pigmented stain has a tendency to cloud the transparency of the dye, so it's advisable to seal the dye with finish before applying the pigmented stain. Sealing the dye allows you to control where you want the pigment to go and makes it easier to wipe off. This process of applying pigmented stains between coats of finish is known as glazing.

## GLAZING

A glaze is a type of thickly pigmented stain that is formulated to be brushed on and wiped off easily. You can buy a colored premixed glaze or a clear glaze medium that you color yourself, or you can make your own glaze. Glazes are different from pigmented stains only by application: Stains are applied to bare wood; glazes are applied between coats of finish. Glazes have an incredible variety of uses but are most effective at coloring pores, correcting the color after finish has been applied, adding an antique effect, and increasing depth.

The simplest glazes to use are pigmented oil-based stains. If you use one of these, choose one that's slow drying. You can use it as is (after stirring the can), or, if you need a darker color, scrape some of the pigment off the bottom of the can with a spoon after the pigment settles. Water-based, lacquer-based, and fast-dry stains don't work very well as glazes. You can make your own glaze by thinning concentrated colorants like artist's pigments or tinting colors. Almost any pigmented medium can be used as a glaze, but the ease with which you can manipulate it after application, whether or not it "bites" into the finish, and how well it cures is determined by the carrier/binder. The commercial glazes are usually formulated for less bite and more manipulation; they can be purchased as clear or tinted.

Whichever glaze you use, they're all applied in the same general way and always after a coat of finish or sealer has been applied to the wood. Begin by brushing a liberal amount of the glaze onto the surface, and then wipe off the excess with a clean, dry cloth (see

To use an oil-based stain as a glaze, brush the stain liberally all over the surface of the wood.

Wipe off the excess glaze with a clean, dry cloth.

Soften marks from the wiping cloth with a special type of brush called a blender.

the top photos above). How much of the glaze color you should leave on the wood depends upon the effect you are trying to create. To blend the glaze into corners and to soften the wiping marks, use a special type of badger-hair brush called a blender (see the photo above). After drying, the glaze must be sealed in with at least one coat of clear finish. Brush the finish with a light touch so that it doesn't pull off the glaze color. The best feature of glazes is their reversibility—if you don't like the color, you can wipe it off with the thinner for the glaze.

# Tinting Colors

In addition to premixed stain and dye powders, there are several other useful colorants. Although some of them can be used to make stains, the main use for these colors is to fine-tune the color of premixed or neutral products.

## Artist's colors (oil/acrylic)

Artist's colors are paints, but they can be used as stains or glazes if thinned to the right consistency. They are much brighter and more vivid than wood stains and are manufactured to exacting standards. The colors can be added to pigmented stains, wood fillers, and glazes. Use the correct medium—oil for oil-based products and acrylic for water-based.

## Japan colors

Japan colors are very finely ground pigments similar to artist's colors. They are oil-compatible only. Use like the artist's colors above.

## Universal tinting colors (UTCs)

UTCs are compatible with water, oil, and lacquer. Use to fine-tune almost any medium except shellac.

## Dry pigments/Fresco powders

These dry pigment powders can be added to any medium because they have no carrier/binder. They are very versatile and are used extensively in repair work.

*Glaze as pore colorant* Some dyes, particularly water-soluble dyes, do not color pores very effectively. After sealing the dye with a coat of finish, apply the glaze to the surface and wipe it off across the grain of the wood to work it into the pores. Once the glaze is dry, apply finish to seal in the glaze. This technique works particularly well with open-pored woods like oak or ash.

*Glaze as color corrector* Glazes can be used to manipulate a color or darken it. For example, use a green glaze to decrease red, a red glaze to increase red, or a dark brown glaze to darken the color. The best glazes to use for color correcting are artist's colors or concentrated tints like Japan colors thinned to a wiping consistency with mineral spirits (see the sidebar above). Brush the glaze on, and then quickly wipe it off so that only a thin veil of color remains.

*Antiquing* Here a glaze is wiped on and wiped off creatively so that it remains only in certain areas such as moldings, corners, crevices, and carved areas (see the photo on the facing page). Commercially prepared glazes work the best for this technique because they dry slowly and are easy to manipulate.

*Increasing depth* Thin pigmented glazes applied over a contrasting base color give an illusion of great depth. Increasing depth was the original use for glazing in oil painting and was

Glazes can be used to create various effects. The pine door on the left was antiqued by leaving dark glaze in the recesses of the beading. The oak panel in the center was glazed to emphasize the pores. The rails and stiles of the pine panel on the right were glazed to equalize the color with the center panel.

perfected by artists like Rubens and Titian. Try applying a red glaze over a yellow-dyed base to create various effects of orange. A very deep and rich green can be created by applying a blue glaze over a yellow dye. Deep, rich browns are obtained by staining the wood with an amber dye, and then applying various dark brown glazes.

## Filling the Grain

All woods have vessels in their cellular structure for the conduction of sap when the tree is living. When the wood is cut into lumber, these vessels are cut, much like straws cut at an angle. The size and distribution of these cut vessels, or pores, are what give many hardwoods their individual character. Pores can be small and hard to see, as in cherry, maple, and poplar, or large and clearly visible, as in ash, oak, mahogany, and walnut.

What you do with the pores during the finishing process largely determines the overall aesthetics of the finished piece. Applying a stain and finish to woods with large pores leaves the pores open (called an open-pored finish). The pore depth is still visible when the wood is viewed at certain angles. When the pores are filled, the wood surface is completely smooth and flat when viewed at any angle (called a filled-pore or a "piano" finish). When the pores are filled and the finish is buffed to a high gloss, a mirrorlike surface results, as seen on high-end furniture and musical instruments like guitars and pianos.

Whether or not you fill the pores is a question of how you want the wood to look. Filling the pores does not add any protective qualities but it does affect tactile and visual qualities. Woods don't necessarily look any "better" when the pores are filled, but filling the pores lends a more formal, elegant look (such as French polish), whereas unfilled pores have a more "close-to-the wood," natural look (such as an oil finish).

### PASTE-WOOD FILLERS

Paste-wood fillers, which may be oil-based or water-based, are comprised of a bulking agent, a binder, and a carrier. In all paste-wood fillers, the bulking agent is the material that fills the pores. It needs to be an inert substance with minimal shrinkage; very finely ground silica, called silex, is the most widely used bulking agent. As in a pigmented stain, something needs to hold the bulking agent in the pores and to itself. The binder is a finish resin, either oil/varnish or acrylic/urethane. The carrier is the solvent compatible with the resin. Mineral spirits is used with the oil/varnish resin and water with the acrylic/urethane resin.

Paste-wood fillers are available in neutral, which is the natural color of the ingredients. Neutral fillers bulk the pores without contrasting them with the color of the flat grain between the pores. Colored paste-wood fillers are also available; they have a colored pigment ground into the mixture, which can blend in with the color of the wood or add a contrasting effect. You can purchase a neutral filler and tint it with dry pigments or a tinting medium compatible with the filler. Water-based fillers can be tinted with dry pigments (sometimes called fresco powders), universal tinting colors, and artist's acrylic colors. Oil-based products can be tinted with dry pigments, universal tinting colors, Japan colors, and artist's oil colors.

### APPLYING OIL-BASED FILLERS

Oil-based fillers are the easiest to apply, but they're not without problems if handled incorrectly. The most common problems are waiting too long for the filler to dry before removing the excess, not letting the filler dry long enough, and leaving application marks under the finish.

Oil-based fillers should be thinned to the consistency of thick cream. Manufacturers usually say on the can whether or not the filler needs to be thinned. Thin fillers are easier to apply and clean off than stiff fillers. Use naphtha to thin the filler.

Work the filler into the pores of the board with a stiff-bristle brush.

Scrape off the excess filler with a rubber squeegee.

Using a piece of burlap, rub across the grain.

Apply the filler with a stiff-bristle brush. I use an inexpensive polyester brush with blunt edges or an old, worn-out black bristle brush. Apply the filler liberally to the surface in any direction, working it into the pores of the wood with the tip of the brush (see the top left photo above). On large surfaces, it's best to work with small, manageable areas until you get the feel for how fast the filler dries. Immediately after brushing, take a rubber squeegee or a thin piece of stiff cardboard and scrape off the excess filler at a 45° angle to the grain of the wood (see the top right photo above). This step is important, because it packs the filler into the pores.

After scraping off the excess, wait for the filler to haze over. Hazing can take anywhere from five minutes to 20 minutes, depending on temperature and humidity. As soon as the filler hazes, take a piece of burlap about 12 in. square, fold it into a pad, and start rubbing off the excess filler from the surface. Work across the grain or at a 45° angle (see the bottom photo on p. 67). Avoid rubbing with the grain because you'll pull the filler out of the pores. Switch to a clean area of burlap when the surface loads up and continue rubbing until no filler shows on the burlap. Then lightly rub the surface in a figure-eight pattern. This motion removes and evens out any cross-grain lap marks from the filler, which would be visible once the finish is applied. Any filler that has dried hard can be removed by squirting a small amount of naphtha on the burlap; the naphtha softens the varnish binder to make removal easier.

Let the filler dry at least 12 hours and then examine the surface. Large-pored woods like oak may need a second application of filler; smaller-pored woods like walnut usually need only one application. Apply the filler as described above if a second application is necessary.

Many problems are caused by not letting the filler dry long enough. Two days is a minimum. In humid weather or cold shops, wait at least a week. After the filler is dry, lightly sand the wood in the direction of the grain with 320-grit stearated sandpaper. Go lightly to avoid cutting through to the bare wood. Rather than using a sanding block, I fold the sandpaper into quarters (see p. 33) and back it up with the palm of my hand. A problem that finishers can run into at this stage is that they think the filler hasn't dried because it gums up the sandpaper. This happens because the fillers are formulated with linseed oil to aid in the application and scraping off. Linseed oil does not dry hard like varnish—it's much softer and flexible so it gums up the paper.

### APPLYING WATER-BASED FILLERS

The general procedure for applying water-based fillers is the same as for oil-based fillers, but with some variations. Water-based fillers dry very fast and can only be removed by sanding. Brush on a liberal coat of filler, and then immediately remove the excess with the squeegee. Don't wait for water-based fillers to haze. After scraping, wipe the board with burlap, across the grain at first and then switching to figure eights. You probably won't be able to remove all the filler because it dries so fast, but don't worry because you'll remove it with the next step. Wait at least an hour, and then sand off the dried filler with 240- or 320-grit stearated sandpaper. If the paper gums, the filler hasn't dried fully; wait another hour and then try again. The filler should powder easily.

Water-based fillers differ from oil-based fillers primarily in that they take certain stains after application; oil-based stains do not. This means that you can use a neutral water-based filler on raw wood, remove the bulk of it, and sand it flush to the surface of the wood after an hour. You can then apply a stain (alcohol-soluble and NGR dye stains are best) to color the wood and the filler. If you use a straight water-based stain, it colors only the wood. Wait at least three hours (but no longer than 12 hours) to apply the stain. Water-based fillers are dry enough to top-coat with finish after three hours. Any finish can be used—water-based, shellac, lacquer, varnish, or polyurethane.

## VARIATIONS IN TECHNIQUE

Colored paste-wood fillers color the wood as well as the pores. There are several ways to control the overall color of the wood when using fillers. One way is to apply filler and stain at the same time. If the color of the filler doesn't quite match the overall color that you want, you can add some compatible stain to the filler. Don't add too much, or the filler will be to thin and require a second application. The best colors to add are concentrated tinting colors or artist's colors. This technique is hit-or-miss, so you have to experiment on scraps to get the right color.

The best technique for controlling color and creating special effects is by staining first, sealing, and then applying filler. This technique works best with oil-based fillers because it's easier to wipe the excess off the sealer coat. Water-based fillers are difficult to remove completely from a sealer coat. The process is similar to glazing, except that the pores are being colored and filled as well. You can create some very dramatic effects this way, because the pores can be a contrasting color to the flat grain between the pores.

Using a stain, establish the color of the flat grain (the area between pores). When the stain is dry, seal it with a coat of finish. When the finish is dry, very lightly scuff-sand it with 320-grit stearated sandpaper. Apply a colored paste-wood filler according to the instructions above. When the filler is dry, remove all the excess by lightly sanding with the grain of the wood with 320-grit paper. Then apply the finish of your choice. If the color still isn't right, you can fine-tune it further with a glaze (see p. 64).

# 4

# Shellac Finishes

In the historical context of finishing wood, shellac is not a particularly old finish. As a finishing material, shellac made its debut in this country around 1820 and slightly earlier in Europe. Prior to that time, shellac was harvested for the red dye contained in the raw material. The resin that was left over had little commercial importance. When aniline dyes were first synthesized in 1856, the shellac dye industry was wiped out. However, methods in refining and purifying the raw resin led to its widespread use by almost all woodworking industries up to the 1920s, when it was replaced by nitrocellulose lacquer.

Shellac is very versatile and well suited to application by hand. It can be applied and polished at the same time (as in French polishing), padded on with a rag, or brushed. Shellac dries fast, does not have a disagreeable odor, and is nontoxic when dry. The dried film rubs out well and can be easily repaired if damaged. Its only drawbacks are that it is marred by strong alcoholic beverages, alkalis (like those in household cleaners), and heat. In spite of these shortcomings, shellac finishes have proven themselves as good-looking, durable finishes for over 170 years.

In this chapter, as in the finishing course that I teach, I'll cover French polishing first. Although the process may initially seem complex, the method I use is really not that difficult to master. Padding shellac, a simplified version of French polishing, and brushing shellac are discussed at the end of the chapter.

# What Is Shellac?

Shellac is an organic resin derived from a tiny bug (called *Laccifer lacca*) about the size of an apple seed. During its reproductive cycle the bug alights and feeds off the sap of certain species of trees indigenous to India and Thailand. The cocoon it secretes to protect its eggs is the raw material for shellac. The cocoons are shaken off the trees and harvested as sticklac. The sticklac is washed and further refined by hand or mechanical means to produce various grades of shellac, which can be processed further for specific needs. Grades include seedlac, buttonlac, #1 orange, Kusmi blonde, and bleached white (see the photo below).

Shellac grading is complex because shellac has varied commercial applications, most of which have nothing to do with finishing. For woodworkers, the two most important qualities are color and wax content. All shellacs have a natural wax as part of the product, but the wax can be removed by filtration. Wax in the shellac reduces its resistance to moisture and makes the liquid finishing material look cloudy in the container, though the cloudiness isn't noticeable in the dried film on the wood. The natural color of the shellac depends on the type of tree, the time of year, and the region where the shellac was harvested. This color can range anywhere from very light amber to dark reddish brown. The light, clear shellacs should be used on woods where little color from the finish is desired. The darker shellacs impart a color that looks good on woods like walnut, cherry, and mahogany.

### MIXING SHELLAC

I like to make my shellac solution from dry flakes; mixing the shellac myself guarantees a fresh solution that will dry properly. In addition, there's a wider variety of colors and dewaxed shellacs to choose from if you use dry flakes. Premixed shellacs are available

Shellacs in dry form include (clockwise from top) seedlac, buttonlac, dewaxed pale, bleached white, #1 orange, and dewaxed dark.

only in #1 orange and white shellac, which is decolorized by chemical bleaching.

The ratio of dry flakes to alcohol is called the cut and is based upon a given quantity of shellac dissolved in a gallon of alcohol. For example, a 2-lb. cut is 2 lb. of shellac dissolved in a gallon of alcohol; a 5-lb. cut is 5 lb. dissolved in a gallon. Since a gallon is usually too much to mix up at a time, I use a smaller ratio; ¼ lb. of dry flakes to a quart of alcohol yields a 2-lb. cut, which is the most common cut used for finishing. It can be diluted further for specific needs.

The best alcohol to use with shellac is denatured alcohol, which is ethyl alcohol that has been made unfit for human consumption by the addition of small amounts of poisonous chemicals. Commercial denatured alcohol that lists "shellac reducer" as one of the uses can be used without problems. Many finishers and

## The Shelf Life of Shellac

Shellac is a natural resin that is composed of complex organic acids. These acids react with alcohol in a chemical process known as esterification. The products of this reaction ultimately turn the normally hard shellac resin into a softer, gummy resin that won't dry. The reaction is gradual, and it takes time to render the shellac useless. I've used shellacs as old as several years successfully, but you should always test them first. Place a drop of the shellac solution onto a glass or metal surface. After 15 minutes, the shellac should be dry to the touch. After overnight drying, scrape the surface of the shellac with your fingernail. If it gums up, it's bad and should be discarded.

The shelf life of shellac in dry form varies depending on storage conditions and the grade of shellac. Over time, dry shellac will polymerize with itself, forming different molecules that will not dissolve in alcohol. Dry shellac that is past its shelf life leaves a jellylike mass at the bottom of the jar that refuses to dissolve—even after a week or so. Don't confuse this with wax that settles to the bottom of the jar with a waxed variety of shellac. If you suspect that the shellac is old and you just bought it, contact the supplier for a replacement or refund.

Both mixed and dry shellac benefit from proper storage. Store dry flakes in the refrigerator or in a cool, dry area until you mix them

up. If flakes are exposed to prolonged periods of hot/cold cycles, the shelf life is shortened significantly. If you order dry flakes that were shipped in hot weather, they may arrive in a caked form; this is called blocking, and as long as it happens only once it should have no effect on the long-term storage life of the flakes. Store the mixed solution in a cool, dry area and try to avoid hot/cold cycles as with the dry flakes.

If you use a premixed shellac, buy one with a guaranteed shelf life from the manufacturer. This way, you have something to fall back on in case the shellac is suspect. Premixed shellacs can be tested as explained previously.

conservators worry about these products because they can contain up to 5% water as well as the poisonous chemicals that are not disclosed to the user. These finishers and conservators use either reagent-grade anhydrous ethanol or pure grain alcohol. Both of these products are acceptable, but they are expensive and in my finishing career I've never had a problem with denatured alcohol that's specified for shellac reducing.

Methanol is sometimes recommended as a good reducer for shellac flakes. It will dissolve shellac just as well as ethanol, but it is much more toxic and the vapors will pass through filters on cartridge-style respirators. There's no reason to use it.

To dissolve shellac flakes, weigh the appropriate amount and add it to the measured amount of alcohol. Use a glass or plastic jar with a tight-fitting lid. Do not use metal containers because shellac is naturally acidic and will discolor by reacting with the metal. Periodically shake the shellac to prevent a jellylike mass from forming at the bottom of the jar. Placing it near (but not directly on) a warm heat source speeds up the process.

Shellacs that have a natural wax content such as #1 orange, buttonlac, and seedlac appear cloudy in solution. This cloudiness is normal and doesn't affect the clarity of the finish. If you wish, you can let the wax settle to the bottom of the jar and decant the clear shellac off the top. Unrefined shellac like seedlac and buttonlac must be strained before use to remove impurities. Dewaxed shellacs such as Kusmi blonde should dissolve into clear solution with no wax residue at the bottom. Dry shellac that's past its shelf life may not dissolve fully, even after several weeks (see the sidebar on the facing page).

# French Polishing

French polishing is arguably the most elegant finish that can be done by hand. Before the introduction of shellac in Europe in the early 1800s, the favored method of finishing furniture to a high gloss was to apply beeswax in thin layers with a cloth and then polish it up to a high gloss. However, wax finishes did not wear well and were easily damaged by water or abrasion. The technique of applying shellac by rubbing it onto the wood with a cloth pad is generally thought to have begun between 1810 and 1820 in France, and its acceptance as the favored finish for fine furniture spread quickly to Britain and throughout the rest of Europe. In France, fine pumice stone was sprinkled onto the wood surface and then ground into the pores with a cloth pad so that a glass-smooth finish could be obtained. In Britain, polishers used gypsum or chalk mixed with various dry pigments to fill the pores. In both methods, a clear coat of shellac was then built up on the wood, which resulted in a finish of great depth and clarity.

## MATERIALS

In addition to shellac flakes and denatured alcohol (see pp. 71-73), other materials used in French polishing include pumice, oil, and a cloth polishing pad.

***Pumice*** Pumice is very fine volcanic glass. In powdered form it is white, but because of its low refractive index, it is transparent when combined with mediums like shellac and oils. When mixed with shellac, pumice makes a transparent "filler" for the pores of the wood. Pumice is an abrasive so it is graded according to particle size. The finest grade, 4F, is used in French polishing.

***Oil*** Shellac is applied with a pad in very thin coats over a number of days. To keep the pad from sticking to the freshly applied shellac, small amounts of mineral oil are put on the surface of the pad. When used in small amounts, the oil will not affect the durability of the shellac film and can be removed easily in the final stage of polishing. The most readily available mineral oil is baby oil, which is a low-viscosity mineral oil combined with small amounts of perfume.

## Making a Polishing Pad

1. Place a golf-ball-size piece of core cloth in the center of a 10-in. square of cover cloth and wet it with ½ oz. of alcohol. Then add a thimbleful of 2-lb. cut shellac.

2. Fold the bottom two corners of the cover cloth over each other.

**Polishing pad**  The pad used in French polishing consists of two parts, an inner core cloth and an outer cover cloth. The traditional products used were flannel or wool for the core cloth and linen for the cover cloth. Linen was used because it does not contain lint, which can get stuck in the sticky shellac as it's being applied. Linen can be hard to find in the correct type so I recommend muslin, which can be purchased at any fabric store. Muslin is graded in stitches per inch—I recommend 80 to 90 stitches per inch, which is sometimes sold as sheeting. Before using the muslin, it's necessary to "de-lint" it and remove the sizing from the fabric. Wet the fabric thoroughly in warm water and wring it out. Dry it on medium heat in a clothes drier to remove the lint.

The inner core cloth can be wool, flannel, or any cloth that will absorb the shellac and alcohol used during the process. I've used old socks, cheesecloth, and cotton with success.

To make a French-polishing pad, wad up a golf-ball-size piece of core cloth and place it in the center of a 10-in.-square piece of cover cloth. Wet the core cloth with approximately ½ oz. of alcohol, wring out any excess, and then add a thimbleful of 2-lb. shellac (one good squirt from the bottle). Fold the two bottom corners of the cover cloth over the core and then bring the two top corners over. Twist the excess at the top to tighten the cover cloth over the core cloth so that a smooth, wrinkle-free surface is left on the bottom. There should be no creases.

3. Then bring down the top corners.

4. Twist the loose ends to tighten the cover cloth around the core cloth.

5. There should be no seams or creases at the bottom of the pad.

A cleat screwed to the underside of this candlestand top will hold it securely during the polishing process.

You can make smaller pads for smaller surfaces or special pear-shaped pads for getting into tight corners and moldings (see p. 87). After using a pad, store it in a glass jar with an airtight lid to keep it from drying out.

In addition to the above items, you need containers to dispense the alcohol and shellac in small amounts. Plastic squeeze-type bottles with spouts work best; they come with caps to cover the spouts when not in use. Have separate bottles for alcohol and shellac.

## THE PROCESS

French polishing is divided into three stages—filling the pores, bodying, and clearing. The process described here is based on the French method, but with one significant variation. The traditional process calls for sprinkling pumice after a light coat of shellac and then grinding it into the wood to fill the pores. This step is tricky and can cause a lot of problems for beginners. The method outlined below entails premixing shellac and pumice and applying it in a method similar to using a paste-wood filler.

The complete process of French polishing is usually done on tops, but you can do it on sides and other surfaces if desired. Secondary surfaces like the undersides of tops and the insides of carcases should be sealed with at least one application of a 2-lb. cut shellac. Brush the shellac on liberally, and after an hour or so, it should be dry enough to handle.

The basics of French polishing should be practiced on flat tops first. As you gain skill in the technique, you can move onto more complex surfaces (see pp. 85-88). The process involves a great deal of pressure on the top, so devise a way to hold it securely. A cleat screwed to the underside works best (see the photo at left).

If you plan on staining the wood, use a water-soluble dye stain or a chemical stain. These stains penetrate more deeply than other stains, and you are less likely to abrade through the stain when filling the pores with the shellac/pumice paste. They are also much easier to fix if you do sand through the stain. Simply reapply some of the original stain with an artist's brush and it will blend in perfectly.

***Filling the pores*** Filling the pores is the first step in creating a perfectly smooth and reflective surface. Begin by vacuuming the surface thoroughly to remove any sawdust. Then make a very thick cut of shellac by adding 4 oz. of shellac flakes (by weight) to 4 oz. of alcohol. I use #1 orange, but you can use any of the grades for subtle color variations. It may take several days for the flakes to dissolve completely. Stir the mixture occasionally (every four to six hours) to prevent a thick mass of partially dissolved shellac from forming at the bottom. When the flakes are fully dissolved, stir in 3 oz. to 4 oz. (by volume) of 4F pumice powder.

An optional step at this point is to put a very small amount of linseed oil on the surface of the wood. The linseed oil increases the depth of the finish. Apply only enough oil to give the surface a "wet" look—don't flood the wood with oil. Then rub the oil into the wood briskly with a soft cloth (see the top left photo below).

## Filling the Pores

1. To increase the depth of the finish, rub some linseed oil sparingly into the surface of the wood before applying the shellac/pumice paste.

2. Work the shellac/pumice paste into the surface of the wood with a stiff bristle brush.

3. Scrape off the excess paste with a rubber squeegee.

4. Wipe any remaining paste off the surface, switching to a clean part of the cloth as it loads with the paste.

Immediately after applying the oil, work the shellac/pumice paste all over the surface of the wood with a stiff bristle brush (see the top right photo on p. 77). Use a small cloth for the edges. Working quickly before the shellac starts to set, scrape the paste into the pores of the wood across the grain with a rubber squeegee. Try to remove the excess paste as cleanly as possible and wipe it off on a cloth before the next pass. Once you've removed as much of the excess paste as you can with the squeegee, wet a clean cotton cloth with alcohol and, using a circular or figure-eight motion, wipe any remaining paste off the surface of the wood. Avoid rubbing the surface with the grain; otherwise, you'll pull the paste out of the pores. Turn the cloth frequently to expose clean cloth as it loads with shellac, and add more alcohol if the cloth dries out.

**In preparation for polishing, charge the bottom of the core cloth with shellac.**

**Glide the polishing pad across the surface, and lift it up as you get to the edge.**

When the pad starts to slide smoothly over the surface, you've removed enough excess filler. Examine the surface of the wood with backlighting. The pores should be mostly filled with the shellac/pumice mixture, and the surface sheen of the wood should have a frosted look. If the pores are large, as in rosewood, ash, and some mahogany, you may need a second application. Woods with small, indistinct pores, like maple and cherry, fill quickly. When you're finished, let the surface dry overnight.

The next day, lightly scuff-sand the surface with 320-grit stearated sandpaper, using your hand to back the paper. If you break the surface on stained wood, reapply more stain and allow it to dry before proceeding. On edges and moldings, use a maroon-grade abrasive pad to avoid cutting through the sharp edges.

Next make a polishing pad as described on pp. 74-75. Pull the cover away from the core and load the core with shellac (about ½ oz.). Apply the shellac to the part of the core cloth that contacts the bottom of the pad (see the top photo on the facing page). Then add an equal amount of alcohol to the same spot. Adding the alcohol thins the 2-lb. cut to a 1-lb. cut, which is used in the initial stages. Alternatively, you can mix a separate 1-lb. cut and use it at this stage. Wrap the cover cloth back over the core and pull it tight. Starting at one end of the board, bring the pad down onto the surface of the wood and glide it across the entire width. Lift the pad up as you get to the other end (see the bottom photo on the facing page). Bring the pad in from the other end and make another stripe back to the starting point, overlapping the previous one by half its width. Continue this process from the top to the bottom of the board. Repeat the process in the same way three or four times until the surface has a thin, even coating of shellac.

**Apply a drop or two of mineral oil to the bottom of the pad to prevent it from sticking.**

### POLISHING SEQUENCE FOR FRENCH POLISHING

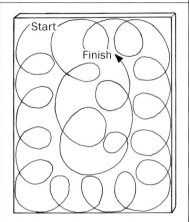

*Work from the outer edges in toward the center of the board.*

Wipe several thin coats of shellac on the edges of the top (for molded edges, see p. 88). Each time you recharge the pad during the subsequent stages of polishing, remember to redo the edges. Once you have achieved a thin coating of shellac on the entire top, you can begin moving the pad in a small circular pattern around the surface of the top. The pad will probably start sticking immediately, so apply one or two drops of mineral oil on the surface of the pad (see the photo on p. 79). Starting at the top of the board farthest from you, work the pad in a circular pattern, moving it around the edges as you form the circles. When you finish the outer edges, bring the pad into the center of the board (see the drawing at left). As the pad moves across the surface, the mineral oil will leave a trail, or a "cloud" as it's called. This cloud is normal and will evaporate a few seconds after it appears; it signifies that you have the correct amount of oil on the pad.

Beginning polishers often run into trouble at this point. As you move the pad over freshly applied shellac, the shellac must be dry enough so that the pad doesn't pick it up, or "burn" it. Move the pad slowly enough so that by the time you get to the point where you started, the shellac has set enough to take another thin coat. Keep the pad moving—if you stop for even a fraction of a second, the pad will stick to the shellac and make a mark. If the circle you make while working the edges reaches the center of the board, you can keep working the board this way. If not, as you work your way around the board, make sure to do the center section also. Change to a figure-eight pattern occasionally to ensure that every part of the surface gets covered with shellac.

As the pad dries out, recharge it with shellac and alcohol. When you start polishing after recharging, use very light pressure on the pad, and then increase it as the pad dries out. Keep examining the surface with backlighting as you work. You may notice that some

**The type of circular pattern you polish with is determined by the size of the board. Make sure that the circle favors the edges and use larger circles (and larger pads) for larger boards.**

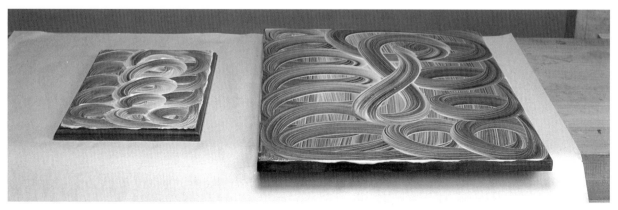

Sprinkle a pinch of 4F pumice between the core cloth and the cover cloth to speed up the process of filling the pores during the bodying stage.

areas do not have the same coverage of shellac. This is because you have a natural tendency to neglect certain areas with your polishing sequence. Turn the board 180° and continue to polish. Work the top until the pores appear filled with shellac (on open-pored woods) or the surface has a shine (on closed-pored woods). Store the pad and let the finish dry overnight.

**Bodying**   After the finish has dried, you may notice that the pores that seemed filled the night before are now visible. Don't be alarmed—it's normal for shellac to shrink as it dries. Using a small amount of naphtha or mineral spirits as a lubricant, lightly sand the surface of the shellac with 600-grit wet/dry paper. Use your hand as a backing block to avoid cutting through the thin shellac. A light sanding is all that's necessary—just enough to knock off imperfections and to even out the surface. The direction in which you sand is unimportant as long as you're putting more finish on top of the surface. Wipe off the residue with a soft cloth.

Now charge your pad with shellac. You don't want to add any alcohol during this stage; using the 2-lb. cut will build faster. Start polishing in circles, switching to figure eights as necessary. As the pad dries out, recharge with shellac. Keep working the edges as before, building the center section as necessary. Add oil only when necessary. The objective at this stage is first to build the shellac until the pores appear filled, and then to build shellac until you can discern a visible thickness to the film. This process may take 15 minutes to 45 minutes, depending on the size of the surface and the size of the pores. If the pores aren't filling, you can speed up the process by sprinkling a pinch of pumice between the cover cloth and the core after charging it with shellac (see the photo above). Adding the pumice turns the surface of the cloth into a very fine abrasive pad, allowing it to scrape off dried shellac and force it into

**In the final stages of bodying, increase the pressure on the pad.**

the pores. When you're satisfied with the shellac build, put the pad away and let the surface dry overnight.

The next day, examine the surface. If the pores are completely filled and the top appears as one level surface, you can proceed to the next step. If the pores are still visible, repeat the previous step. Keep repeating the bodying process until the pores are no longer visible after overnight drying. This may take two or three days, depending on how large the pores are and how well you filled them during the filling stage.

When you're satisfied that the pores are filled, make a new pad and charge it with shellac. Place a drop of oil on the work surface and begin polishing. This time when the pad dries out, don't recharge it. Instead, increase the pressure until you are polishing with an almost dry pad. There should be resistance or friction

## Clearing the Shellac

1. Bring the pad down lightly on one end of the board.

2. Glide the pad across the surface.

Make a clearing pad by wadding up a palm-size amount of padding cloth with no creases on the bottom. Charge the pad with enough alcohol to dampen it slightly.

between the surface of the pad and the shellac, but not so much that the surface is marred. Add oil if necessary. Using as much pressure as you can, work the surface of the board until a deep, even gloss appears (see the top photo on the facing page). What you are doing is burnishing a gloss onto the surface of the shellac with a dry pad. Move the pad slowly and deliberately until there are no pad marks or other imperfections.

**Clearing**   Clearing removes the oil used during the polishing process from the surface. It's important that the shellac be dry, so I like to wait several days before clearing. Make a pad by wadding up some padding cloth or fresh cheesecloth, as shown in the photo above. It should have no creases on the bottom. Squirt a little alcohol onto the pad and work it in so that the cloth is slightly

3. Keep the pad moving so that it doesn't stick.

4. Lift the pad off the board as you reach the opposite end.

# Open-Pored French Polish

If the high-reflective surface of French polish is too glossy for your taste, you may find an open-pored version more appealing. Rather than filling the pores as described in the text, go right to the bodying stage. Then build up the surface exactly as described. This results in a glossy, but open-pored look (it's sometimes called an open-pored French polish). The open pores interrupt light, and the surface appears less reflective. You can build up the surface as much as you like, or leave it with a minimal amount of shellac.

Note that if you've polished the surface in the conventional manner and it's still too glossy, you can cut down on the sheen by rubbing with 0000 steel wool or a fine rubbing compound.

damp (it should feel like the tip of a dog's nose). If you can wring out alcohol, it's too wet.

Bring the pad down very lightly on the surface of the shellac (see the photo essay on pp. 82-83). "Kiss" the surface with the pad and keep it moving briskly back and forth over the surface. The pad should glide easily and not stick. Change to a clean part of the pad frequently so that it will continue to pick up the oil. As the pad dries out, apply more pressure and use a buffing motion, going back and forth with the grain of the wood. Continue this process until you have a rich, deep gloss.

## PROBLEMS WITH FRENCH POLISHING

Several problems can arise during the polishing process. Listed below are the most common ones and ways to correct them.

***Burning***   Burning occurs when you wipe the pad across shellac that hasn't set up enough and the pad picks off the finish. It's tempting to fix the problem by wiping on more shellac in the affected area, but this only exacerbates the burning. Stop and let the surface dry for 30 minutes or longer. Very lightly abrade the burned area with 600-grit wet/dry paper, using several drops of mineral spirits as a lubricant. Continue polishing, but do not favor the damaged area. If you ignore it and continue normal polishing, it will correct itself.

Burning can also occur on small surfaces. The center gets over-worked and begins to burn because every time you make a small circle to work the edge, you are hitting the center as well. To remedy this problem, make a smaller pad and slow down your polishing speed. Changing your polishing pattern more frequently helps, too.

***Shellac doesn't build***   Shellac doesn't build when you get too much oil on the surface during the bodying stage. The correct amount of oil leaves a discernible trail behind the pad as you move it across the surface. It should evaporate in a matter of seconds. If you have too much oil, the trail will not evaporate. To remove the excess oil, let the board dry 10 minutes or longer, then wipe the surface lightly with a clean cotton cloth dampened with naphtha. Make a new pad since the cover cloth is probably saturated with oil.

***Shellac turns white***   Shellac turns white when the relative humidity is very high (90% to 100%). Many times the white spots will disappear if you leave them alone, but, if not, make a fresh clearing pad and lightly wipe the whitened area with alcohol until the white marks disappear. Of course, if you want to avoid the problem of shellac turning white altogether, it might be wisest to find other things to do than finishing on days with high humidity.

**Sweating**   Sweating shows up as tiny beads of oil that form on the surface after drying overnight. It is caused by using too much mineral oil in the initial stages. The oil is absorbed into the wood and "sweats" out later. Wipe the beads off with naphtha and a clean cloth.

**Small holes**   Tiny depressions and holes may appear as you build a surface film of shellac. These defects are most noticeable around inlays. To fill the holes, use a toothpick to drop in a small amount of the shellac/pumice mix (from the filling stage). Don't try to smooth the filled area. Let the mix dry until it's hard enough to slice off with a very sharp chisel, and then sand lightly with 600-grit wet/dry paper before continuing.

**Adjusting color**   As you build the shellac, you may find that you want to alter the color slightly. You can control the color to a certain extent by selecting the right color shellac in the first place, but sometimes you may want to cool down a red tone or even out sapwood/heartwood differences. On antiques, you can darken sun-bleached areas to match the rest of the piece. The best way to adjust the color without stripping and starting over is by adding small amounts of an alcohol-soluble dye to the bodying shellac. Only a little dye should be used; if you use too strong a solution, lap marks will appear that are impossible to even out. Since all dyes vary in concentration, it's hard to recommend a ratio of dye powder to shellac, but I usually dissolve a half-thimbleful of dye powder in an ounce of alcohol first, and then add it in small amounts to the shellac solution. Strain the solution before using. Build the color change slowly. Use a dilute green solution to cool a red tone or subdue an orange tone. Various reds and browns can be used to darken areas and blend in sapwood.

An alternative, though more difficult to control, technique is to add varying amounts of mixed dye (without shellac) to the pad, and then dilute with a squirt of shellac. By working this way, you can vary the intensity of the color more effectively.

## POLISHING COMPLEX SURFACES

Once you've gotten the hang of polishing flat surfaces, you can move on to more complex polishing situations. Below are some of the most common.

**Turnings**   Turned objects can be French-polished while they're still on the lathe. With the tool rest removed and the lathe running at around 1,700 rpm, hold a small pad with some linseed oil or tung oil to the surface of the spinning work. Then use a small, clean

**To fill the pores of a turned leg, hold a pad with shellac/pumice paste against the spinning work.**

cloth to burnish the oil dry. Take some of the shellac/pumice paste in a small cloth and hold it to the surface of the spinning work, moving it slowly from one end to the other as many times as needed to fill the pores (see the photo above). Switch to a clean cloth and, using a 2-lb. cut shellac, spin the shellac mixture onto the surface, again working slowly from one end to the other. Add oil to the pad if it starts to stick. Make several passes, and let the shellac set slightly after each pass. Turn the lathe by hand to spirit the oil off the turning.

*Safety note:* It is extremely important to use as small a pad as possible and to hold it under the spinning work when French-polishing on the lathe. Rags with frayed edges or a loose weave should not be used.

**Corners and right angles**   To polish corners and right angles, you'll first need to make a small, pear-shaped pad. This pad is made in much the same way as a standard polishing pad (see pp. 74-75), except that the core material is a long roll rather than a ball. Place

# Making a Pad for Polishing Corners

1. Place a roll of core cloth in the center of the cover cloth.

2. Roll the corners over the core, maintaining a point at the tip.

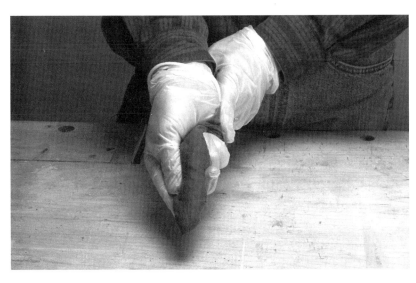

3. Twist the loose ends to make a pear-shaped pad.

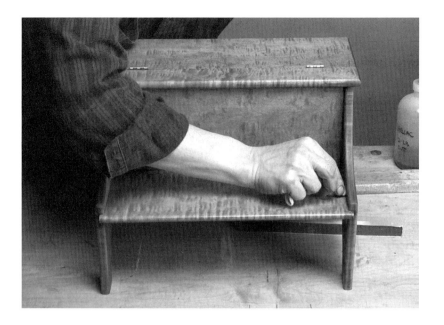

**Work the very tip of the polishing pad into the corner, keeping the pad moving at all times.**

the core cloth in the center of the cover cloth and roll the corners over, maintaining a point at the tip (see the photos on p. 87). Then twist the loose ends at the back to form a pear shape.

Work the very tip of the pad into the corner as you polish, trying not to stop the pad or overwork the area. Keep the pad moving by polishing out into the center areas, then coming back in to hit the corner again. This motion gives the shellac time to dry. The most common problem is trying to overwork the corner to make it perfect, which usually results in the burning problem described on p. 84.

*Moldings*   Moldings are polished using the padding-shellac technique described on pp. 89-93. Using padding cloth or trace cloth, make up a pad and squirt some 2-lb. cut shellac on the surface. Bring the pad down onto the molding lightly, and then increase the pressure to make it conform to the contours. As the polish builds, add a drop of oil to the surface of the pad to keep it from sticking.

**MAINTAINING A FRENCH-POLISH FINISH**

There are two ways to maintain the deep gloss of a French-polish finish. The best way to restore the surface shine is to go through the clearing process again. If the surface is dirty, wipe it lightly with a clean rag and naphtha before clearing. If the surface gets damaged by heat, scratches, or liquids, you can restore it by wet-sanding with 600-grit wet/dry paper and mineral spirits followed by a quick

To polish a molded edge, wad up a small piece of padding cloth and dispense some 2-lb. cut shellac onto the bottom surface. Use pressure to make the pad conform to the molded edge as you wipe on the shellac.

bodying, then clearing. If there are scratches, fill them with several applications of a 2-lb. cut shellac applied with an artist's brush. Wet-sand lightly between applications, and then continue with bodying until the scratches disappear.

If repeating the clearing process is inconvenient or you've finished the piece for a client, an emulsion furniture polish works fine (see pp. 167-168). The polish should be wiped gently over the surface until the gloss is re-established.

## Padding Shellac

If the process of French polishing seems a little daunting, there is an easier application method, known as padding shellac. This technique produces comparable results, although the finish surface is not as highly reflective as with French polishing. Where the technique of padding shellac originated is unclear, but it seems likely that it was in this country. I know many cabinetmakers who still use this process to apply shellac. The main difference between padding shellac and French polishing is that no filler other than shellac is used to fill the pores. In many cases the pores can be left unfilled or only partially filled, depending on the look that you are trying to create. The cloth used to apply the shellac is different, and no oil is used to lubricate the pad. The surface can be left gloss, satin, or flat depending on the sheen you want to rub out to.

## MATERIALS

The only materials needed for padding are a lint-free padding cloth, 2-lb. cut shellac, and tung oil or linseed oil.

The best cloth for applying shellac by this method is manufactured from bleached, 100% cotton; it is sold as padding cloth or trace cloth. The cloth should be absorbent and as lint-free as possible. Avoid T-shirts or dyed material.

Make a 2-lb. cut shellac solution from fresh shellac flakes, as described on pp. 71-73. Drying oils like tung or linseed oil can be used as a sealer coat under the shellac to increase depth and figure. If you use linseed oil, make sure it is boiled linseed oil.

## THE PROCESS

Prepare the surface to the desired grit, and stain if desired. The best stains to use for this application are fully cured oil-based pigmented stains, water-soluble dyes, or chemical stains. These three colorants have less chance of pulling off the surface with the pad. Other coloring materials will pull off with the initial padding technique and lighten considerably.

Padding is much easier on flat, unobstructed surfaces, so I recommend that you refrain from gluing up until you have padded on several applications of shellac. This technique works particularly well with case pieces. Mask off all surfaces that will be glued, and use plugs on mortises or dadoes.

***Applying the oil*** Apply about a thimbleful of oil per square foot with a clean pad (you can omit this step on wood stained with a pigmented oil stain). Use just enough oil to make the surface of the wood look wet; avoid flooding it with oil. Rub the surface briskly. If you apply oil to case insides, drawers, or any surface that gets

Padding is much easier on flat surfaces. Wait to glue up until after several coats of shellac have been applied.

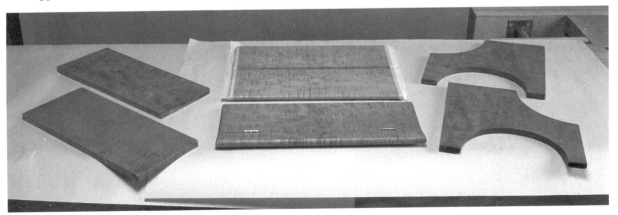

closed off from open air, allow at least one week's drying time. Otherwise, the smell of the oil will linger when the piece is glued up. I usually refrain from oiling areas that aren't visible, just to be safe.

**_Padding the shellac_**    Use enough padding cloth to make a pad that will fit comfortably in your hand. A 10-in.-square pad will fit small hands, and a 15-in. square pad will fit larger hands. Fold the cloth into a flat ball so that the bottom surface has no seams or wrinkles. (If you have to pad an inside corner, make a pad with an "ear" on the end so that you can work it into tight places.) Pour approximately 1 oz. of denatured alcohol onto the pad and work it in. Squeeze the pad to force out excess alcohol, and then pour about ½ oz. of a 2-lb. cut shellac onto the bottom surface of the pad.

Dispense 2-lb. cut shellac onto the bottom surface of a padding cloth that's been wet with denatured alcohol.

Wipe the shellac on in stripes down the entire surface of the board.

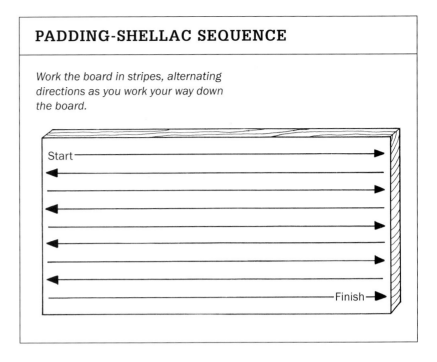

**PADDING-SHELLAC SEQUENCE**

*Work the board in stripes, alternating directions as you work your way down the board.*

Start

Finish

To apply the shellac, start at one of the top corners. Working with the grain of the wood, bring the pad down lightly, wipe a stripe of shellac across the board, and then gently raise the pad up and off the other side (see the bottom photo on p. 91). Reverse directions, coming in from the other side, and repeat the same motion. Keep working the board from top to bottom in this striping fashion until you get to the bottom (see the drawing above), and then wipe the edges. If there's a complex molding, make the pad conform to the shape of the molding (see the photo on p. 89). If you miss a spot, don't try to wipe it because you'll pull up the shellac around it. By the time you reach the bottom of the board, the top should be dry enough to wipe again. Repeat the process, taking care to cover any spots you may have missed the first time. Recharge the pad with more shellac when it dries out. Keep padding until the finish feels tacky and the pad starts to stick. Let the first coat of shellac dry at least one hour.

Using 320-grit stearated paper, lightly scuff-sand the surface. Scuff sanding is exactly as it sounds—you sand lightly enough so that you just scuff the surface of the finish. Afterward, smooth out the surface with a maroon-grade synthetic abrasive pad. Apply a glaze if you want to add depth or change the color, and allow it to dry. The best glaze to use is an oil-based stain because, after thorough drying, it will have less of a tendency to pull off with the subsequent padding. Repeat the padding procedure until you get an even coating of shellac on the surface. Use very light pressure if you've applied a glaze, to avoid picking up too much of the color on the pad. If you haven't glued up your project, now is the time to do so. You can wipe off glue squeeze-out if you want, but I like to let the glue dry for 30 minutes, then pull it off like tape.

The next day, rub out all surfaces with 320-grit stearated paper and the maroon-grade abrasive pad. Apply another coat of shellac to all surfaces and let dry overnight.

At this point, the surface should have an even coating of shellac. On porous woods, you'll see the crisp outlines of the pores, which is appealing if you want a close-to-the-wood look. For tops and other surfaces that receive a lot of wear and tear, you may want to apply several more padding applications of the shellac. When building thicker shellac films, it's not necessary to sand between coats, but allow at least six hours' drying time between applications. Stop when the finish depth is what you want. Let the finish dry before proceeding to the next step.

**Rubbing out**   Rubbing out the shellac results in a smoother, better-looking finish. Wait at least two days before rubbing out. To be sure the shellac is ready, press your fingernail into the finish; if it marks easily, wait longer. Unlike brushing (see pp. 96-99), padding leaves virtually no marks or irregularities in the finish, so rubbing out goes quickly. Lightly scuff-sand the surface with 400-grit stearated paper. Then rub the surface thoroughly with 0000 steel wool, using paste wax (or a rubbing lubricant like Behlen's Wool-Lube) as a lubricant. Thin the wax 50/50 with mineral spirits to make application easier. On dark, open-pored woods, use a dark wax so that the residue that gets stuck in the pores won't be visible. When the wax is dry, buff for a satin sheen. If you want a higher gloss, use dry steel wool after the 400 grit, and then switch to 4F pumice and rottenstone to raise the gloss before waxing. Apply the wax with a cloth instead of steel wool.

**Maintaining a padded finish**   Wax imparts a satiny sheen that is quite attractive, but it does not affect the durability of the shellac finish. A yearly rewaxing will keep the finish looking great. Avoid placing hot objects on the surface and alkaline household cleaners like ammonia. If scratches or other marks appear, a light sanding with 400 grit followed by repadding and rubbing out repairs the finish.

White marks can be repaired by removing wax with naphtha and then rubbing the offending area with a clearing pad dampened with alcohol. To blend it in with the rest of the finish, rub out with steel wool and rewax.

# How Durable Is Shellac?

Shellac was the favored finish for the furniture industry up until the late 1920s and 1930s when it was replaced by nitrocellulose lacquer. Since then, lacquer has become the benchmark finish in terms of durability and good looks. To compare the durability of shellac, I finished three panels: one with dewaxed pale shellac, one with water-based lacquer, and one with solvent lacquer. I then conducted a simple series of tests to compare solvent resistance, water resistance, heat resistance, and scratch resistance (see the chart on the facing page).

## Resistance to alcohol, solvents, and household chemicals

Three reagent ethyl-alcohol concentrations were placed on the panels for five minutes: 100%; 50% alcohol, 50% water (duplicating a strong alcohol like whiskey); and 10% alcohol, 90% water (duplicating wine). Drops of acetone, mineral spirits, vinegar, and ammonia were also left on the panels for five minutes.

## Resistance to water

All three panels were subjected to water by placing three ice cubes on the surface and letting the water melt and then sit overnight on the panel.

## Resistance to heat

Hot tap water (150°F) was poured on each of the panels, and then a coffee mug was placed on the water for five minutes. Any impression from the mug was noted. The test was repeated using boiling water (212°F).

## Resistance to scratching

The panels were scratched with pencils of varying hardness. I used six pencils: 6H (hardest), 4H, 2H, H, B, and 2B (softest).

As you can see from the tests, shellac's biggest enemies are alcohol, alkalis (ammonia), and heat. Lacquer fares the best for all-around durability, but what surprised me was that shellac and water-based lacquer were almost equivalent in all the tests. Water-based lacquer was comparable to shellac in resistance to alkalis and alcohol, but it was softer in the scratch test. The traditional complaint against shellac—poor resistance to water—isn't valid if dewaxed shellac is used. Boiling water was needed to affect the shellac. All alcohol solutions above 10% damaged shellac, but the water-based lacquer was dissolved by the 100% and deglossed by the 50/50 blend.

# Durability Tests

| Test | Shellac | Water-Based Lacquer | Solvent Lacquer | Remarks |
|------|---------|---------------------|-----------------|---------|
| Alcohol (100%) | F | F | F | Solvent-lacquer mark not as deep as others |
| Alcohol (50%) | F | F | P | Equivalent to whiskey, vodka, etc. |
| Alcohol (10%) | P | P | P | Equivalent to wine |
| Acetone | F | F | F | Dissolved all finishes |
| Mineral spirits | P | P | P | |
| Vinegar | P | P | P | |
| Ammonia | F | F | P | Household ammonia (5%) |
| Cold water (12 hours) | P | P | P | |
| Hot water (150°F) | P | P | P | |
| Boiling water (212°F) | F | P | P | Outline of mug visible on shellac |
| 6H | V | V | V | |
| 4H | V | V | V | |
| 2H | S/V | V | S/V | |
| H | S/V | S/V | S/V | |
| B | N/V | N/V | N/V | |
| 2B | N/V | N/V | N/V | |

P = pass (no damage noted); F = fail (damage visible); V = visible; S/V = slightly visible; N/V = not visible

## Brushing Shellac

French polishing and padding are possible with shellac because of its rapid drying time. However, there may be situations where you can't apply shellac with a pad, such as on carvings or other complex surfaces. When refinishing, complete disassembly of the piece is not possible, so you may be faced with corners, right-angle joinery, and turnings, all of which are problematic to finish with a pad. In these situations, brushing is more practical.

The rapid drying time of shellac can be a disadvantage when it comes to brushing. Any problems that occur during the brushing process are hard to correct because the shellac sets quickly. If you try to go back and correct a mistake, you'll probably make it worse. Brushing shellac demands a very controlled technique and the right tools. On the plus side, brushing shellac is the most efficient application method. You can apply more finish in one application than is possible with padding or French polishing.

### MATERIALS

When brushing shellac, use a good-quality natural or synthetic brush. Fitch brushes, high-quality white China bristle brushes, or synthetic-bristle brushes are all good choices for brushing shellac on large, flat surfaces. For intricate and complex surfaces, I recommend an artist's brush made from a synthetic filament called Taklon. All the brushes mentioned have very fine, soft bristles, so brush marks are minimal.

The cut of the shellac should be determined by the surface you're brushing. A 2-lb. cut is the best cut to start with for brushing large, flat surfaces. As you gain experience with the brush, you can move up to a 3-lb. cut. If you have problems with the shellac not flowing out, or if there are brush marks when it's dry, you have two choices. Switch to a lighter cut or add a retarder to the shellac. Any retarder for solvent lacquer will work with shellac. Add about ½ oz. to 1 oz. per quart of mixed shellac solution. Retarders extend the drying time, so you may have to add several hours' extra drying time between coats. (To check if the shellac is dry enough, lightly scuff-sand with 320-grit sandpaper: If it powders, it's dry enough; if it gums up the sandpaper, it needs to dry longer.) Reduction of the shellac from 2 lb. to 1½ lb. also helps. To convert a 2-lb. cut to a 1½-lb. cut, add 10 oz. alcohol to every quart of the 2-lb. cut shellac solution.

## BRUSHING TECHNIQUES

Brushing technique varies slightly depending on whether you're working on a flat surface or a more complex surface.

*Flat surfaces*  Arrange the work so that you have backlighting, either from a lamp or natural light. Dip the brush into the shellac halfway up the bristle length. Pat the brush against the inside of the jar or can to remove excess shellac. Starting about 3 in. in from the edge, pull the brush toward the edge (see the top photo below), lifting it up lightly when you get to the edge to avoid drips. Come back to where you began, and then work the brush quickly in long, quick strokes to the opposite edge (see the bottom photo below). Try not to overload the brush with shellac to avoid creating pools and uneven finish thickness when the shellac dries. Overlap each brush stroke slightly, and continue down the board until you have it covered. Do the edges last.

When brushing a flat surface, start a few inches in from the edge to avoid drips (above), brush toward the edge, and then bring the brush back the other way, working quickly toward the opposite edge (right).

Don't attempt to smooth out the shellac you've just applied since this will pull up the partially dried film and wrinkle it. If you miss a spot, forget about it, and cover it with the next application of shellac.

The first application of shellac goes on easily and dries evenly because most of the finish is absorbed by the wood. After one hour, the shellac is usually hard enough to scuff-sand in preparation for the next coat. Use 240- or 320-grit stearated sandpaper and lightly sand off the raised wood fibers.

Apply the second and subsequent coats in exactly the same way as the first one. (How many coats you apply is up to you, but no protective qualities are gained beyond three or four coats.) Sanding between coats isn't necessary unless there are bits of debris, drips, or thick pools from brushing. Prior to application of the last coat, dry-sand the shellac as level as possible using 240- or 320-grit stearated sandpaper backed by a cork block. Take your time applying the last coat over this level surface.

**Complex surfaces**   When brushing complex surfaces, I recommend using a synthetic-bristle artist's brush for better control. These brushes hold less finish, so you should change your technique slightly. I also use a lighter-cut shellac (1 lb. to 1½ lb.).

**Brush turnings with a round-and-round stroke, quickly feathering the shellac into the previous strokes.**

When brushing a right angle, start at the inside angle and work out toward the edge.

On carved surfaces, brush the shellac briskly into the carvings and wick out the excess by holding dry bristles in the shellac. You can "highlight" raised areas by reapplying second coats to these areas. On turnings, work the shellac on in a round-and-round brush stroke, feathering out the shellac as quickly as possible (see the photo on the facing page). Load less shellac on the brush to avoid runs and drips.

Using a square-tipped artist's brush really helps in corners and right angles. Lightly load the brush with a 1½-lb. cut and work out from the corner (see the photo above). Try not to pool the shellac by overloading the brush, and feather the shellac quickly to blend it into the rest of the finish.

## RUBBING OUT

Brushed shellac finishes should be rubbed out just like padded shellac finishes (see p. 93). The only difference is that you may need to spend more time with the initial leveling step to even out surface irregularities from the brushing application. Rub out with wax or a rubbing lubricant for a satin finish or 4F pumice and rottenstone for a higher gloss. (For more on the process of rubbing out, see pp. 126-130.)

# 5

# Oil Finishes

*Oil* is an all-encompassing term that refers to a wide range of products. When used in the context of finishing wood, an immediate distinction should be made between oils that dry and oils that do not dry. Linseed oil and tung oil are examples of oils that dry, or convert from a liquid to a semisolid state when exposed to air. The ability to dry is the single most important characteristic of these oils, and it is why they have wide applications in finish formulations. Mineral oil is an example of an oil that does not dry. It remains in liquid form when exposed to air.

Oils are probably the oldest known finishes used to protect wood. Since they are natural products derived from plants and trees, they are easy to obtain and process into a form suitable for applying to wood. They can be applied easily without adding other ingredients like thinners. Mixed with pigments, they make paints. Eventually, methods were discovered to process the oils, resulting in more durable and protective coatings. Oils are still widely used and are the backbone of the paint and varnish industry. As yet, no synthetic material has been developed to equal drying oils in cost and overall performance.

The great appeal of oil finishes is that they are easy to apply and they impart a very pleasant depth and surface luster to the wood. The allure and mystique of the traditional, hand-rubbed linseed-oil finish are well known. In this process, the finisher would rub linseed

Oil finishes add depth, accentuate figure, and increase surface luster, as seen on this freshly oiled curly-maple and walnut tabletop.

oil into the wood once a day, using the palm of the hand. The process was repeated faithfully every day for several weeks (sometimes months) until the legendary glow appeared on the surface of the wood. Manufacturers of finishing products realized the marketing potential of this type of finish but knew that a speedier process was needed to sell their products. Formulations began to appear that mixed oil with varnish or polymerized oils. These finishes build more quickly, allowing satisfactory results to be obtained in days rather than weeks.

## Types of Oil Finishes

Of the many products advertised as oil finishes, only a few can legitimately be called pure oil finishes. These are linseed oil and tung oil, either raw, boiled, polymerized, or oxidized. These two oils, blended with other products, form the bulk of the finishes sold as oil blends.

### LINSEED OIL

Linseed oil is derived from the seeds of the flax plant. Flax is the same plant that yields linen, hence the name *lin*-seed oil. Linseed oil is amber colored and darkens significantly with age. The unprocessed oil is called raw linseed oil. Raw linseed oil cures very slowly, but heating it to very high temperatures speeds up the cure time. In years past, this heated oil was referred to as boiled linseed oil. Today, boiled linseed oil is raw linseed oil that is heated to a much lower temperature and has oil-soluble driers added to it to make it cure faster. Linseed oil builds slowly, and if a surface film of oil is built on the wood, it will be very soft and gummy. It is easily damaged by water.

## TUNG OIL

Tung oil is a relative newcomer to this country. Originally cultivated from the nuts of tung trees native to China, it was introduced to the United States in the early part of this century. Tung oil is lighter in color than linseed oil, doesn't darken as much over time, dries more quickly, and has better resistance to moisture when cured. It is slightly more durable than linseed oil but has a frosted, matte appearance unless multiple coats are applied. Tung trees were planted in this country to harvest the raw material, but nowadays most of the oil comes from South America.

## POLYMERIZED OILS

When linseed oil or tung oil is heated to temperatures between 485°F and 570°F in the absence of air, the oil becomes partially polymerized. This oil is more viscous than the raw oil and is known as bodied, cooked, or polymerized oil. The heat-polymerization process decreases the drying time of the oil significantly and increases the durability. Polymerized oils have been used in varnish formulations for a long time. Pure, polymerized tung oil is available for finishing. Polymerized linseed oil is not available in pure form but is usually found in blends.

## OXIDIZED LINSEED OIL

When linseed oil is heated to around 570°F in the presence of oxygen (air), the oil is known as oxidized linseed oil. The oxidation process makes the oil thicker, decreases the drying time, and renders it capable of producing a semigloss film with good moisture resistance. The only manufacturer producing oxidized linseed oil today is Tried and True Wood Finishes, 14 Prospect St., Trumansburg, NY 14886; (607) 387-9280.

## OIL BLENDS

Oil can be blended with other products to change the characteristics of the dried oil film. Oil blended with small amounts of varnish or polymerized oil is the most common product, and it increases the durability of the finish slightly and allows the finisher to build the finish more quickly. Since linseed oil and mineral spirits are the least costly components, most oil and varnish blends are predominately thinned linseed oil, regardless of what the label says. Many finishers concoct their own "home" brews from these three components (see the sidebar on the facing page). Changing the oil/varnish ratio changes the working qualities of the finish.

Boiled, oxidized, or polymerized oils can also be blended with beeswax. These products have a very attractive satiny appearance but lack the durability of the oil/varnish blends. (The addition of the

# Making Your Own Oil and Varnish Blend

One of the biggest problems with oil blends is that most of the manufacturers have had to re-formulate their products in the last five years to comply with lower VOC (volatile organic compounds) regulations mandated by several states. As a result, products that you loved to use 10 years ago are not the same products today. The solids content and finish viscosity are higher, which affects the physical working qualities of the product and the way it dries.

Many finishers have answered this problem by making their own oil blends. While proportions vary, a good formula to start with is one part varnish, one part oil (tung or linseed), and one part mineral spirits. You can vary the amounts to adjust the working qualities of the finish.

The finish is soft if built up in thick coats, so it's best to apply thin coats; if you want a harder finish, use a wiping varnish (see pp. 124-125). Mixing even a small amount of oil into a varnish changes the hardness of the varnish dramatically.

wax to the oil makes it even less durable than a straight oil finish.) Because of their low-luster effect, these oil/wax blends are a good choice for finishing interior millwork like crown molding and beams.

# Applying Oil Finishes

Oil finishes are favored for the "close-to-the-wood" look that they create. This means that most of the finishing material is in the wood—hence the designation *penetrating* finishes. This term is somewhat misleading because all finishes penetrate to a certain degree. They have to if they are to adhere to the wood at all. Nonetheless, most oil finishes are not built up on the surface, unless they are the polymerized oils or oil/varnish blends that contain a fair amount of varnish. Because the tactile and visual surface of the wood is still evident, surface preparation and staining considerations become very important.

**PREPARATION**
Plane or scrape the wood to the desired smoothness. Careful planing with a razor-sharp blade will yield a shimmering texture under an oil finish. When sanding, go to at least 240 grit. Sand to 180, and then wet the wood with distilled water to raise the grain. After the wood is dry, resand with 240. Surfaces sanded above 320 will appear "shinier" under the initial coats, but this is because the oil isn't penetrating into the burnished wood surface.

Oil finishes work best on unstained surfaces. The major reason not to use a stain is that there is very little finish to protect the coloring, so rub-throughs of the stain layer can occur during most normal wear and tear. In addition, any rubbing of the cured oil finish to change the sheen can easily abrade the stain. Since most finishers are after a natural look when using oil finishes, staining usually isn't a consideration.

If you absolutely have to stain, use a water-soluble dye or a chemical stain. These two stains penetrate the deepest and won't bleed into the oil/thinner mix. You can also add small amounts of an oil-soluble dye or an oil-based stain to the finish.

Filling the grain is a matter of preference. However, I think that a big part of the attractiveness of an oil finish is when the pores are open and the edges around the top are sharply defined. To keep the pores defined, vacuum the wood thoroughly before applying the first oil coat.

### TRADITIONAL LINSEED-OIL FINISH

The traditional linseed-oil finish presented here, which I was taught many years ago, is a time-consuming process that produces a mellow sheen and emphasizes natural graining. It imparts an amber tone to the wood. On some woods, particularly cherry, linseed oil seems to accelerate the natural darkening of the wood, although it's not clear why.

***First coat*** To assist penetration, heat boiled linseed oil over medium heat (around 125°F) to lower the viscosity. *Never heat oil with thinner in it.* The oil should be the consistency of whole milk when properly heated. Flood the surface of the wood liberally with

**Apply hot linseed oil with a synthetic-bristle brush, flooding the surface liberally.**

the hot oil. Use a synthetic-bristle brush because the hot oil will ruin natural bristles. Reapply oil where dry spots appear and let the oil soak in for one hour. Wipe all excess oil off the surface with a rag and let the surface dry for one to two days (the surface of the wood should feel dry when you brush your hand across it).

*Safety note:* Oil-soaked rags are a fire hazard. Wet oil-soaked rags under water and drape them over the side of a metal trash can or use an approved container for oily rags (see p. 8).

**Top coats**   Lightly scuff-sand the surface of the wood with 320-grit sandpaper. Go lightly if you've stained the wood, taking extra care at any sharp corners. Reapply another coat of oil (this time, there's no need to heat the oil). Apply the oil very thinly and evenly and wipe off the excess after it sets for one hour.

Repeat this procedure at least four more times, allowing at least 24 hours between coats. The more coats you build, the deeper the color and depth (see the photo below). Do not apply another coat until the previous one is dry. If the surface feels gummy or tacky, let it dry longer. Longer dry times are usually needed as you build coats, but do not try to build a film of oil as if you were using shellac. Remove all excess oil after each application.

For a silky-smooth surface, wet-sand the final coat of oil while it's still on the wood with 600-grit wet/dry paper (see the photo on p. 106). Don't try this on porous woods—wet sanding muddies the clean, open appearance of the pores. Be extremely careful if you've stained the wood to avoid cutting through to the bare wood. Remove the excess oil with a clean rag and allow the final coat to dry.

Once the final coat is completely dry, there are a number of ways you can adjust the sheen and/or smooth the surface further. To

**The more linseed oil you apply, the deeper the color and better the depth. The left side of the board has three applications of linseed oil; the right side has seven.**

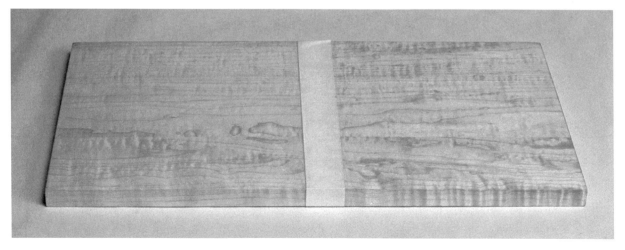

**Wet sanding the final coat of a linseed-oil finish while it's still on the wood leaves a silky-smooth surface when the oil dries.**

raise the sheen of the finish slightly, wrap a piece of cotton T-shirt-type cloth around a cork block or cork-faced wood. Rub the dried oil briskly, with moderate pressure (see the photo on the facing page). This technique works best when the last coat of oil has cured for at least several weeks.

To smooth the surface and decrease the sheen of the finish, rub very lightly with 0000 steel wool. To smooth the surface and raise the sheen slightly, dip the steel wool in paste wax and rub in the direction of the grain of the wood. You can dilute the wax with mineral spirits to make it easier to apply. Buff off the excess wax with a clean cloth when it hazes. Let the wax dry overnight and apply the next coat of paste wax with a cloth pad (see pp. 166-167).

A waxed linseed-oil finish is not very durable, and, although it will make water bead, water left on the surface for any length of time will spot. To repair water damage, dull spots, scratches, or other normal wear and tear, remove the wax with mineral spirits and then sand lightly with 320-grit paper. Reapply more oil, let dry, and then wax again. To maintain this finish, re-oil the surface every two years. Apply paste wax at least twice a year.

### TRADITIONAL TUNG-OIL FINISH

Tung oil can be applied in the same way as linseed oil, but the tung oil will retain a frosted look unless you build up the surface or rub the cured oil (see the photo on p. 108). The color is not quite as

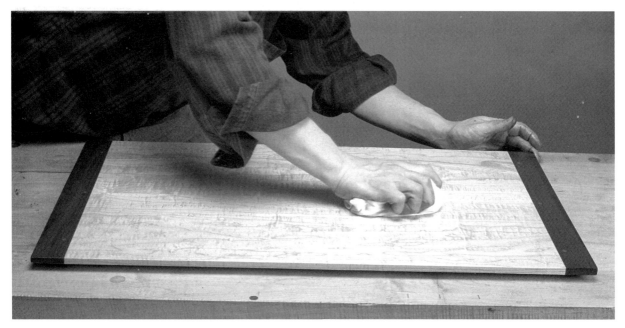

Using a piece of T-shirt wrapped around a cork block, rub the dried oil briskly with moderate pressure.

deep as linseed oil. Tung oil offers better water and chemical resistance than boiled linseed oil but, like any oil, it is soft if built up, so abrasion resistance and stain resistance are minimal. Over time, tung oil tends to require less maintenance than linseed oil.

### OXIDIZED LINSEED OIL AND POLYMERIZED TUNG OIL

Oxidized linseed oil and polymerized tung oil are nice alternatives if you like the look of a traditional oil finish but want quicker results and durability. You can build up these oils on the surface of the wood if you wish, and they dry more quickly than pure oils because they are partially cured by the time they are applied to the wood. (Pure oils reach this point only after a long drying time.) They should be applied in the same way as the pure oil, with slight variations.

***Oxidized linseed oil***   Two coats of oxidized linseed oil look like five or six coats of boiled linseed oil. Subsequent coats build to a semigloss surface, which can be rubbed out to satin. This product dries more quickly than boiled linseed oil, and coats can be reapplied one day apart as long as the temperature is above 70°F. Since oxidized linseed oil is much more viscous than boiled linseed oil it may take a little more elbow grease to apply it, but the dried film provides a hard, moisture-resistant film very quickly.

Boiled linseed oil (left) and oxidized linseed oil (second from left) dry to a semigloss film. Tung oil (right) and polymerized tung oil (second from right) dry to a frosted appearance. They can be rubbed after thorough drying to raise the sheen.

***Polymerized tung oil***  This product is available in different sheens, which are determined by the solids content of the polymerized oil in a mineral-spirits thinner. The higher-luster sheens dry more quickly, so you should apply and wipe them off within the time specified on the product. Most polymerized tung oils need to be thinned 50/50 with mineral spirits for the first sealer coat. The top coats are applied full-strength as thin coats and allowed to dry at least 24 hours; they are then scuff-sanded or rubbed with steel wool before the next coat is applied.

Polymerized tung oil dries much faster and harder than pure tung oil. A finish built up of thin layers of polymerized tung oil has good resistance to water, chemicals, and heat. The dried film can be rubbed with a cloth rag like other oil finishes, but it comes up to a higher luster and sheen. The finish can also be rubbed with fine abrasives like rottenstone to increase the sheen.

### OIL BLENDS

When pure oils are thinned with mineral spirits and then mixed with a small amount of varnish or polymerized oil, the finish will build more quickly and be slightly more durable. Oil blends are known by several brand-name designations, but the most common are Danish oil, Nordic oil, and Watco. These products are predominately thinned boiled linseed oil with a small amount of tung oil (sometimes) and polymerized oil or varnish. The varnish could be either phenolic, alkyd, or uralkyd (see p. 112). The differences in protective qualities would theoretically vary depending upon the amount of tung oil and type of resin in the formulation, but the finish coats are usually thin, so, in practice, differences are hard to prove. The exact type and ratio of oil to varnish in these mixtures are impossible to determine, and manufacturers do not disclose them. Aesthetic differences are apparent if the oil used is predominately tung oil, which does not darken light-colored woods as much as linseed oil.

Using an oil blend is not very different from using other oil products. Apply the finish liberally to the surface of the wood and wipe off the excess after 30 minutes. Reapply oil when dry spots appear. Scuff-sand the surface after one or two days' drying and apply a thin coat of oil, just enough to wet the surface. Let it sit a minute or so, then wipe off the excess. Alternatively, you can wet-sand the subsequent coats of oil before they set, and then wipe off the excess (see the sidebar at right). There is no need to build the finish; it will be soft and not very durable.

**Problems with oil blends**   The biggest problem that can occur with oil blends is "bleeding." Bleeding usually happens with large-pored woods like oak and ash, but it can also occur on wood with smaller pores like walnut and mahogany. The problem is caused by the addition of mineral spirits to the oil. The finish at the very top edge of the pore starts to dry. The still-wet finish underneath wants to "climb" back out because of surface-tension disparities between the dry film at the top of the pore and the wet film at the bottom. There are two ways to combat this problem. You can wipe off the wet rings around the pores as they appear, but this requires vigilance in checking the surface every hour as the finish dries. A better solution is not to flood the surface: Apply several thin coats initially until the pores are sealed.

If the pores bleed and the finish dries in scabs around the pores, you have no choice but to sand off the scabs and apply more finish. Use a backing block to shear off the scabs. You can also use a chemical stripper to remove them.

## Choosing an Oil Finish

Oil finishes have distinct advantages over other types of finishes. Ease of application, subtle good looks, and repairability are big factors in choosing any of the oil finishes mentioned in this chapter. Oil finishes don't leave brush marks or fish-eyes (see p. 126), dust isn't a concern, and, except for bleeding and long drying times, application isn't a problem. Even if you make a mistake, you can usually reapply more oil to fix the problem. Minor scratches and abrasions can be fixed by wiping more oil on the surface. In a nutshell, oils provide some measure of protection without detracting from the true character and texture of the wood.

On the minus side, most oil finishes do not provide a good barrier between the wood and sources of damage. The problem is twofold. Most oils are inherently weak barriers against moisture, heat, and abrasion. To compound the matter, there's little finish as

## Wet Sanding an Oil Finish

This technique (for use with a home-made oil blend) was suggested to me by one of my cabinetmaking friends. Begin by making a mixture of one part pure tung oil, one part mineral spirits, and one part Waterlox Transparent Varnish. After sanding the wood to 320 grit, apply a wet coat of the mixture to the wood. Wait 20 minutes, and then wet-sand the finish with 320-grit wet/dry paper. Wipe off the excess.

After at least 24 hours' dry time, reapply another wet coat of the mixture, let it sit for 20 minutes, and then wet-sand the surface with 600-grit wet/dry paper. Repeat the above steps until the finish builds to your liking. The resulting finish is a silky-smooth, satin sheen, but you can wax it with paste wax after several days' drying if you wish.

**Oil finishes are a good choice for showing off the contrast between the various woods used in this table (curly maple, maple, walnut, and cherry).**

a protective layer between the wood and the source of the damage. For this reason, you may want to choose a more durable film-forming varnish for furniture that gets a lot of wear.

I use an oil finish when I want to accentuate the figure, add depth, and increase surface luster on wood. Many times I use oils under a film-forming finish like shellac or lacquer. The oil allows me to achieve a great sense of depth to the finish, avoiding the "plastic" look that many find objectionable with a thick film-forming finish. Oils are also a good choice to set off differences between contrasting woods, and to accentuate changes in wood grain, like the end grain on dovetails (see the photo below).

The differences between the oil finishes, whether pure oil, polymerized, or oil blends are subtle. Overall, I prefer the warm golden tones of boiled linseed oil; if you don't want to spend two months with boiled linseed oil, try the oxidized version. Tung oil is a good choice where you want to downplay the change in color, as on maple or other light woods. Luster and sheen are controllable by the degree of build, and polymerized tung oil and the oil blends can often be used to achieve certain aged and antique effects. Of all the oils, polymerized tung oil dries the hardest and the fastest, and comes closest to a varnish in durability.

Whichever oil finish you choose, remember one thing. All oil finishes are maintenance finishes, which means that you have to reapply more oil every one or two years. If you do not, the wood surface will gradually oxidize and take on a lifeless look. Reapplying the finish is not usually a problem if it's a piece of furniture for your own use. If it's a project you've finished for a customer, you'll need to educate them on how to take care of an oil finish. Most cabinetmakers give their customers a small can of oil when they deliver the finished piece.

**Oils accentuate the contrast between the face grain and end grain on dovetails (left). A water-based lacquer does not emphasize the contrast as much (right).**

# 6

# Varnishes

For durability and good looks, few finishes can beat an oil-based varnish. Varnish brings out depth and the natural figure in wood. It applies well with a brush or a rag, and, because it dries slowly, is easy to smooth out if you make a mistake. There are a wide variety of varnishes available and most are inexpensive. On the downside, varnish is sensitive to application in extreme weather conditions and difficult to repair once fully cured. Its slow dry time is also a drawback, because only one coat can be applied in a day and dust can settle in the finish as it cures.

## What Is Varnish?

In finishing terminology, the word *varnish* is inexact and throughout history has meant different things. In the broadest sense, it refers to any thin, glossy coating used on wood or other surfaces to protect them. It is thought to be derived from either *vernix*, the Latin word for amber, or *veronix* the Latin word for sandarac, a natural resin produced by certain species of pine trees. One of the oldest documented procedures for making varnish involved heating amber, the hard fossilized resin from extinct pine trees, until it melted, and then adding it to linseed oil.

Historically, varnishes have been divided into two classes. *Spirit* varnishes were those made by dissolving natural resins like sandarac, mastic, shellac, and dammar in turpentine or alcohol. *Oil* varnishes were made by heating a hard natural resin like copal or amber until it was liquid and then adding it to a drying oil like linseed oil or tung oil. Nowadays, all varnishes are based on drying oils and are manufactured using sophisticated chemical processes that use synthetic resins like phenolic, alkyd, and urethane. These are the varnishes sold today under the general grouping of oil-based varnishes.

## CHEMICAL COMPOSITION

All varnishes are made up of four components: resin, vehicle, carrier, and driers.

The resin is the part of the varnish that forms the hard part of the film. Three types of resins are used in most varnishes. Alkyd resins are the most commonly used and offer good all-around durability. Phenolic resins are harder and tougher than alkyds and rub out better. Urethane resins are added to alkyds and have the best resistance to solvents, chemicals, and abrasions.

Resins alone are too brittle to be used as finish, so a vehicle must be added to the resin to increase the flexibility and durability of the varnish. Drying oils like linseed and tung are used in varying proportions as the vehicle. Varnishes made with a high percentage of oil are called long-oil, spar, or marine varnishes; they are elastic enough to handle the large degree of wood movement outdoors. Short-oil interior varnishes are made with a lower percentage of oil. These varnishes are harder and rub out better than long-oil varnishes. Semi-drying oils like safflower and soya are also used as vehicles. These oils are paler in color than linseed and tung.

A carrier is a liquid, compatible with the resin/oil mix, that thins the material so that it can be applied to the wood. Mineral spirits, or thinner, is almost always used today, although turpentine was used originally. The amount of mineral spirits added determines the viscosity of the varnish and whether it can be brushed on or wiped on with a rag. Varnishes with more thinner build more slowly.

Resin/oil combinations normally take a long time to cure, so the manufacturer adds driers to speed up the drying time. You can add your own drier (sold as Japan drier in most paint stores) to the varnish if it dries slowly.

In addition to the four main components, several other ingredients may be added. Flatteners are inert materials such as silica that are added in different amounts to produce semigloss, satin, and flat sheens. Flatteners float to the top of the varnish as it dries, thereby

# How Varnish Dries

All oil-based varnishes dry the same way. The varnish is applied to the wood surface with either a brush or a pad, and the carrier (C) starts to evaporate (see the top drawing at right). How long this takes depends on the evaporation rate of the carrier as well as on the weather conditions.

The resin/vehicle (R/V) mix is still tacky at this point, but it starts to react with oxygen in the air (see the center drawing at right). This reaction (called polymerization) is gradual and may take several hours or days depending upon the chemical composition of the resin/vehicle, the amount of drier added to the varnish, and the air temperature. The colder the air, the longer the varnish will take to dry. Relative humidity has little effect on dry time. The reaction produces a new chemical product—the dried varnish coating (see the bottom drawing at right)— which is why varnish is classified as a reactive finish.

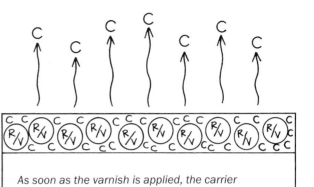

*As soon as the varnish is applied, the carrier starts to evaporate.*

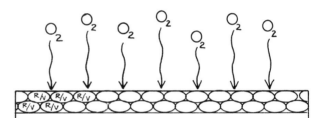

*When the carrier has evaporated, the resin/vehicle mix is tacky, and oxygen begins to react with the mixture...*

*...to form a new chemical compound—the dried varnish film.*

deflecting light at the surface of the dried varnish. Anti-skinning additives are chemical anti-oxidants added to prevent a skin from forming in the can when it's resealed. UV stabilizers are added to exterior varnishes to improve the finish's resistance to ultraviolet light, which can cause cracking, peeling, and discoloration.

All the varnishes made today are variations on the above components. Wiping varnishes (see p. 124) are nothing more than thinned brushing varnishes. Gel varnishes (see p. 125) are wiping varnishes with a gelling agent added so that they can be wiped on with a pad. Rubbing varnishes (see p. 127) are based on short-oil phenolic resin that dries hard and rubs to gloss well.

## Brushing Varnish

Brushing an oil varnish is the traditional method of application. Varnishes formulated for brushing build more quickly than the thinner varnishes for wiping. Usually two to three coats are all that are needed for a durable film. Brushing a varnish successfully requires use of the proper brush, combined with patience and proper technique—a poor brush choice or hurried technique can spell disaster.

### MATERIALS

The best brushes for applying varnish have fine soft bristles with the capacity to hold a lot of finish. The brushes that fit this description are chisel-cut oval China bristle and chisel-cut fitch brushes. A well-made varnish brush is expensive but worth every penny. (For more on brushes, see Chapter 1.)

Varnish selection is not quite as straightforward as brush selection. Your choice of varnish depends on two main factors: where the furniture will be used (i.e., indoors or outdoors) and the degree of rubbing out you intend to do (see the sidebar on the facing page). Note that varnishes with flatteners can be extremely cloudy if several coats are applied. It's better to build up the finish with gloss and apply the last coat in the sheen you want (i.e., flat or satin). Alternatively, finish in gloss and rub out the finish to the desired sheen.

To thin most varnishes, use mineral spirits or the solvent recommended by the manufacturer. Naphtha can be used in place of mineral spirits for a faster drying time. Turpentine will extend the drying time.

# Choosing a Varnish

Fifty years ago, when varnishes were still made from natural resins like copal and dammar, you could walk into any paint store or hardware store and choose from varnishes classified as spar, floor, rubbing, polishing, pale rubbing, table top, coach, bar top, and spraying varnish. As the natural-resin formulations were replaced by the more durable and cheaper-to-produce synthetic alkyds and urethane formulations, many of the descriptive names faded into obscurity.

Today, finish formulators have at their disposal literally hundreds of possible resin/oil combinations. Unfortunately, trying to work out the precise identity of the various varnishes available can be very confusing. Some manufacturers list the resin/oil components, others do not. If the label does not specify the type of resin/oil used, it's probably an alkyd/soya or safflower oil. Tung oil, phenolic resin, and urethane resin are costly, and manufacturers will go to great pains to tout these ingredients on the label, even though they may be present in only small amounts. Once you know what's in the can, the following breakdown should help you select a varnish suited to your application.

**Alkyd/linseed oil** These amber-colored varnishes are good all-purpose varnishes for interior furniture and woodwork, offering good water, heat, and chemical resistance. They rub out to a decent satin sheen, but not very well to gloss.

**Alkyd/soya, safflower oil** These varnishes have most of the characteristics of the alkyd/linseed-oil varnishes, but they are paler in color.

**Phenolic/tung oil** In short-oil versions, these dark-colored varnishes are the equivalent of the old rubbing varnishes that were based on copal. They are excellent varnishes for rubbing out to gloss. Since tung oil dries harder and has better water resistance than linseed oil, long-oil versions are good exterior varnishes (see the sidebar on p. 116). Phenolic-resin varnishes are harder than alkyds and have better resistance to heat and chemicals, but they yellow considerably over time.

**Urethane, alkyd/linseed, soya, safflower oil** Marketed simply as polyurethane, most of these varnishes are standard alkyds to which urethane has been added. Generally, these are the best finishes in overall durability for interior applications, though they are difficult to rub to an even sheen. The urethanes used in most varnish formulations do not have good exterior qualities, so manufacturers may add UV stabilizers to minimize cracking, peeling, and yellowing.

## PREPARATION

Varnish is particularly sensitive to the environment in which it is applied, so be sure to review the information in Chapter 1 before applying the sealer coat. Because varnish has a slow drying time, dust falling into the finish poses a problem. Proper rubbing out can correct this problem (see pp. 126-130), but it's a good idea to keep your finishing area as free from dust as possible. The varnish and the wood should be at room temperature, so do not work in a cold room or unheated garage. Cold air significantly reduces the ability of varnish to dry properly.

# Varnishing Outdoor Furniture

There are no easily applicable clear exterior finishes that will stand up to harsh outdoor exposure for any length of time. Any varnish will start to crack and peel in strong sunlight, so try to arrange your furniture so that it's in a shaded spot or receives a minimal amount of southern exposure. Thick varnish applications will start to peel after several years, and peeling varnish will have to be removed before applying new varnish. I prefer to apply just enough varnish to seal the wood, and then wipe on a new varnish coat yearly after a light scuff sanding.

Before you begin brushing varnish, plane, scrape, or sand the wood to at least 180 grit. Remove the sawdust with a vacuum cleaner, and then wipe the piece with naphtha or mineral spirits to highlight any imperfections (see pp. 39-41). If you want to color the wood, you can use any type of stain under varnish. When using an oil dye, however, be sure to seal the dye with shellac to prevent bleeding (see p. 109).

## SEALER COAT

The purpose of the first, or sealer, coat of any finish is to stop up the pores and to lock the wood fibers in place. For varnish there are three choices for sealer coats: a varnish sanding sealer, thinned varnish, or shellac.

***Varnish sanding sealers*** These are thinned, inexpensive alkyd varnishes that are mixed with zinc stearate, the same chemical that gives stearated sandpaper its anti-loading quality. The stearates bulk up the first coat, so that the next finish coat flows on smoothly and evenly. The stearates also make the sealer coat very easy to sand. Varnish sanding sealers speed the buildup of the top coats, so they are ideal for production situations, but they also have several drawbacks. First, they reduce the clarity of the finish and are similar in appearance to a flat or eggshell varnish. Second, stearates are hygroscopic, meaning they swell during high humidity, which can cause the harder top coat to "craze," or crack, if too much sanding sealer is used.

***Thinned varnish*** If you take the stearates out of sanding sealers, you have thinned varnish. A brushing varnish thinned 50/50 with naphtha or mineral spirits is an excellent sealer for wood. It has better clarity than sanding sealer and freezes the fibers so that they can be sheared off when dry by sanding. On new wood that isn't naturally oily, thinned varnish is the best choice.

***Shellac*** As discussed in Chapter 4, shellac is about as perfect a sealer material as you can use. It has excellent adhesion to wood, and any finish applied over it adheres well, too. It dries fast, and the sealer coat can be sanded after 30 minutes. On naturally oily woods like rosewood and other exotics, shellac seals in the oils that prevent oil-based varnishes from drying. On refinished wood, shellac seals in oils and silicones from polishes and stripper residues. Shellac should also be used to seal in oil-based stains and dyes. Use only the dewaxed shellacs, because oil-based polyurethane could peel away from shellac with wax in it.

***Brushing the sealer coat*** Applying the sealer coat does not demand great skill, but care should be taken to achieve even coverage. After conditioning the brush (see p. 11), dip it into the sealer halfway up to the ferrule and knock off the excess sealer by pressing the tip against the side. Apply the sealer to the secondary surfaces first (such as top undersides and case insides). Brush the sealer vigorously with the grain using the tip of the brush. Don't worry if air bubbles appear in the sealer, because the wood absorbs most of the sealer coat and the bubbles will disappear.

Brushing any flat surface is much more efficient if you use a nail board, which is a piece of ¼-in. plywood with 1-in. to 1½-in. brads placed in the four corners to support the piece. On heavy pieces like large tops, use as many nails as you can to distribute the weight of the board evenly.

After brushing all surfaces, let oil-based sealers dry overnight and shellac at least 30 minutes to an hour. Then sand the surfaces with 320-grit stearated sandpaper, either with the grain or at a slight angle. If the paper gums and clogs quickly, the sealer needs to dry longer. Sand very lightly around the edges, or use a synthetic abrasive pad, which has less of a tendency to cut through sharp edges or complex profiles. If you do cut through the sealer (but not the stain), the top coats should blend right in. When you've finished sanding, vacuum the dust off the surfaces and wipe with a tack cloth.

**With the flat workpiece positioned on a nail board, brush the sealer coat onto the surface with the grain of the wood.**

## TOP COAT

Top coats can usually be applied full strength. Most manufacturers produce a varnish that's the correct viscosity for brushing, although some products may be a little too thick. The ideal viscosity is somewhere between that of whole milk and honey. If necessary, add thinner until the correct viscosity is reached; you rarely have to add more than a capful per cup of finish. Stir the varnish thoroughly, particularly if you're using satin or flat sheen, but not too vigorously that you create air bubbles in the finish.

***Brushing horizontal surfaces*** Brushing a top coat is easiest if the surface is horizontal, so, if possible, reposition any large vertical areas so that they lie flat. Whether or not you apply top coats to secondary surfaces is up to you, but I recommend that you do. Brushing secondary surfaces provides better protection and gives you the chance to judge the viscosity of the finish as well as the performance of the brush; you can make corrections before brushing primary or visible surfaces.

I usually finish interior surfaces that show, like the insides of cases and drawers, with one top coat after the sealer. I finish the backs of doors with the same number of coats as the front. On tables with delicate turned or carved legs, I apply one light top coat; too much finish obscures delicate details. There aren't any hard-and-fast rules about how much finish to apply except one: The top always gets the most critical attention, so focus your best brushwork there. I finish tops with at least three and sometimes four or five coats, depending on the viscosity of the varnish.

The basic brush stroke for top-coating is as follows. Condition the brush by dipping it up to the ferrule in mineral spirits or

**When applying top coats, start about 3 in. in from the edge to avoid drips and runs.**

naphtha and wring out the excess. Dip the brush into the varnish halfway up to the ferrule, let it sit for a second or two, and then take the brush out at an angle. Let the excess finish fall off the end of the brush. Starting 3 in. in from the left or right edge, draw the brush toward the edge with the grain of the wood (see the photo on the facing page). Lift it slightly just before it clears the edge to avoid drips. Now, bring the brush back to where you started and flow the varnish on in a straight stroke toward the other edge. Flowing varnish on is a difficult technique to master at first because most of us are used to sloshing the brush back and forth as if painting the side of a house. Move the brush slowly and increase the pressure slightly toward the end of the stroke to dispense the varnish. If dry spots start to appear, reload the brush. If small bubbles appear, leave them alone for now. Also leave alone any large puddled areas that may appear where you begin your stroke. Work the whole area this way, overlapping each stroke slightly until the surface is covered with varnish. Then do the edges.

To even out the finish and remove most of the air bubbles, you need to "tip off" the varnish after you've brushed the whole surface. Remove excess finish from the brush by scraping it along the top edge of the can. Then hold the brush at a 90° angle and drag it lightly over the surface from edge to edge in straight lines with the grain (see the photo below). Scrape off the excess finish again and repeat until you've covered the whole board. Examine the board carefully with backlighting to check for puddles and missed areas. Recoat if necessary and then tip off. The board should now have an even coating of varnish. There may be small air bubbles and ridges from brush marks, but they should disappear as the carrier evaporates. Trying to work the finish to remove every tiny air

**After brushing the entire surface, "tip off" the varnish to even out the finish and to remove air bubbles.**

When working on a vertical surface, brush the finish on horizontally (left), and then tip off vertically (right).

bubble or speck of dirt will only exacerbate the problem. Set the piece aside in a warm, dry area out of the way of dust.

Some varnishes have a fast-drying carrier that can evaporate before you're done tipping off, and the brush may start to stick. To extend the open time of the varnish, add a small amount of turpentine, which evaporates more slowly than mineral spirits.

**Brushing vertical surfaces** Vertical surfaces that can't be repositioned to lie flat require a technique called cross-brushing, which entails brushing on the finish horizontally and tipping off vertically to eliminate sags and drips. A heavily loaded brush causes runs and sags at the beginning of a stroke on vertical surfaces so dip only the tip of the brush into the finish. Start at the top or bottom approximately 3 in. in from the edge and brush toward the edge. Now come back in the other direction toward the opposite edge. Since the brush is not as loaded, you may need to replenish it with finish more often, but try to avoid large sags or drips. If you see a drip, wipe it off with the brush and work the area again. Once the entire surface is covered, tip off from the bottom to the top to even out sags and smooth the varnish. As a final step, wipe under the bottom edge with a rag to remove any varnish runs.

If you're brushing a vertical frame-and-panel side, "cut in" the inside edge of the panel first with a small brush. I like to use a 1-in. China bristle or fitch rectangular chisel brush. Then cut in the inside edges of the rails and stiles. If finish pools in the corners, wick it out with a dry brush or clean cloth. Then complete the rest of the side as described above.

**Brushing complex surfaces**   Brushing a complex surface like a frame-and-panel door requires patience and preparation. Most problems can be eliminated and the varnishing process speeded up with the use of a nail board. Make a nail board with the nails positioned so that they support the door at the four corners. Place the door face down on the nail board and brush the back of the

## Brushing a Frame-and-Panel Door

1. With the door resting on a nail board, cut in the back of the raised panel first.

2. Finish the rest of the back, and then flip the door over.

3. On the front of the door, brush the deepest parts first.

4. Finish by brushing the rails and stiles and the field of the raised panel. Do the edges last.

To varnish a turned piece, brush round and round the turning with a lightly loaded brush and then tip off lengthwise.

door, cutting in the back of the raised panel first. Don't brush the edges. Pick up the door by the dry edges, flip it, and set it down on the nails. (The small holes left by the nails will be invisible after the finish cures.)

Now cut in the inside edge of the panel, and then brush the molded edge of the rails and stiles. Next brush the raised field and the rails and stiles. When you tip off, do the vertical stiles last. Finish the door by brushing the edges, using a small brush to prevent varnish from crawling over to the other side. If you see a drip, pick it up with the brush and then work the area again.

Turned pieces can be a challenge to varnish because they're not easy to tip off. Dragging the brush at a right angle to the sharp portions of the turning guarantees a drip. The best way to finish turnings is to use a gentle round-and-round motion with a lightly loaded brush (see the photo above), and then tip off lengthwise, being careful to hop over any sharp edges.

**Small items like knobs are easiest to brush on the nail board.**

On carved and intricately detailed areas, I don't recommend brushing on a full-strength second coat. I find that a second coat thinned 50/50 dries thin enough to maintain the detail.

Small items like knobs can be difficult to brush. They should never be brushed while attached to the drawer; instead, stick knobs down on one of the nails on the nail board and use a small artist's brush to apply the varnish.

### ADDITIONAL COATS

The application of a third coat of varnish maximizes the durability of the finish. I always apply at least three top coats to tops since these areas get the roughest treatment as well as the most critical attention. If the design of your piece dictates that the sides or other surfaces be finished the same as the top (as on a piano), apply additional top coats to these areas, too.

The previous top coat must be dry enough to recoat. Most varnishes dry sufficiently overnight, but drying time can vary depending upon temperature, the type of varnish, and the amount of drier added to the varnish. To check if the varnish is dry, lightly scuff-sand it with 320-grit stearated paper in an inconspicuous area. If the paper gums easily, let the varnish dry longer.

When the varnish is dry, lightly sand all surfaces with 320-grit stearated sandpaper wrapped around a backing block to knock off all the dust specks and pimples in the finish. Then rub the surface all over with a maroon-grade synthetic abrasive pad (see p. 31) to create a smooth, level surface for the next coat to bond to. Wipe all surfaces perfectly clean with a tack cloth. If there is a lot of dust, vacuum it with a brush attachment first. Then brush the second top coat on as you did the first.

For a super-smooth finish on tops, wet-sand with 320-grit wet/dry paper before applying the final coat. Using a backing block and soapy water as a lubricant, sand the varnish until the entire surface has a dull, frosted look and there are no ridges or low spots. Low spots appear as glossy areas when you start sanding because the sandpaper hasn't reached those areas. Brush aside the slurry frequently to check your progress, and be careful not to sand too much or you'll go right through to the bare wood. Wipe the surface with naphtha to remove any last traces of the soapy water.

## Wiping Varnish

If you thin a brushing varnish to the consistency of whole milk, you have a wiping varnish. Just like brushing varnish, it can be long-oil or short-oil, predominately tung oil or linseed oil, and based on alkyd, phenolic, or urethane resin. Some brands add a thixotropic agent that gels the varnish, making application easier. Most wiping varnishes aren't precisely identified, and some are disguised as oil/varnish blends (for example, Danish oil). Since it can be hard to tell what you're buying, I prefer to thin brushing varnish in the ratio 2 parts thinner to 1 part varnish. (You can vary this ratio to adjust the working qualities of the finish.)

Wiping varnishes are easier to apply than brushing varnishes, and the finished surface is smoother and free of marks. The only drawback is that the finish is thinner, so it takes longer to build to the same thickness as a brushed varnish. Also, since the coat is thin, it's easy to rub through the final coat when rubbing out (see pp. 126-130). Otherwise, wiping varnishes are a very attractive alternative to brushing.

### APPLYING WIPING VARNISHES

The best cloth to use with wiping varnishes is a clean, lint-free padding cloth (the same kind used for padding shellac). An alternative is cotton T-shirt type cloth, but make sure to wash and dry it first to remove the lint. Pour some of the varnish into a

When using wiping varnishes, wipe the varnish on with a pad in any direction. Finish up with long, smooth strokes with the grain of the wood.

shallow pan or dish (a tuna can is ideal). Make a small pad from the cloth and wipe the varnish onto the surface. You can wipe in any direction, but be sure to end up with long, straight strokes with the grain of the wood. Let each coat dry overnight. A very light scuff sanding with 400-grit stearated paper is recommended between coats; after sanding, remove dust with a tack cloth.

Wiping varnishes can be built to any thickness, so the number of coats you apply is up to you. As with brushing varnish, the final coat on the top of a piece should be your best, so take your time and use a backlight to make sure you've covered the whole surface. Finish up all applications with long smooth strokes that cover the whole length of the top.

For complex edges and moldings, use a small pad and conform it to the shape of the profile as you work. Finishing carvings is next to impossible with a pad, so use a small brush instead.

## GEL VARNISHES

Gel varnishes are wiping varnishes that have a gelling agent added to make them thixotropic, meaning that the gelled substance converts to a liquid when energy is applied. These varnishes are very easy to use and are applied like the wiping varnishes just described. Because gel varnishes don't drip or run, precise application is possible and they are excellent for complex pieces like raised panels and turned legs. For carvings, apply gel varnish with a soft-bristle toothbrush (see the photo at right). The downside of gel varnishes is that they are usually more expensive than brushing and wiping varnishes, so I use them only on hard-to-finish items.

Gel varnishes are ideal for finishing complex surfaces like carvings. Here, the author works the varnish in with a soft-bristle toothbrush.

# Troubleshooting Varnish Problems

The best techniques and materials don't always eliminate problems with varnish. Here are some common problems you may encounter, along with ways to correct them.

**Fish-eyes** Fish-eyes are craters that form in the varnish because oils and waxes containing silicone are still in the wood. This problem commonly occurs with refinished pieces. If craters form, immediately wipe off the varnish with mineral spirits and allow the wood to dry. Seal the wood with a 2-lb. cut shellac, let dry, and revarnish. If craters still form, add a fish-eye additive to the varnish (available from H. Behlen & Brothers, 4715 State Highway 30, Amsterdam, NY 12010; 518-843-1380).

**Runs and sags** Deal with runs and sags as they occur, smoothing them out by tipping off. Try to catch runs and sags while most of the carrier is still in the varnish.

If the carrier has evaporated but the finish is tacky, don't try to fix a drip. Wait for it to dry and slice it off with a very sharp chisel. Then sand the area to feather the drip into the surrounding finish before applying another coat.

**Finish doesn't flow out** Flow-out problems can occur when the finish is too thick or when the room, project, or finish is too cold. Varnish flows out best at 70° to 90°F, so keep the finish and the finishing room within this range. Warm the varnish by placing it in a pan of hot water. Never heat varnish directly in the can. Be careful not to heat varnish too high since this makes it set too quickly off the brush and prevents tipping off. If the varnish is still too thick after warming, add a little thinner.

**Varnish won't dry** This problem is caused either by cold temperature or by using a varnish that has little if any drier added by the manufacturer. Warming the room or adding Japan drier will speed up the drying process.

**Dust specks** Large dust specks or other debris can be picked out of the varnish with a sharp toothpick or dental pick before all the carrier has evaporated. Don't worry about smaller specks—rubbing out will take care of them.

**Air bubbles** If small bubbles are still in the film after tipping off, ignore them, since most of them will disappear. If there are lots of bubbles or large ones, they may have been in the varnish before you brushed it or they may have been caused by brushing the varnish too vigorously. Large bubbles can be pierced with a sharp pick. If bubbles are a recurring problem, it may be easier to wipe off the varnish and reapply it using the correct technique or change the varnish.

# Rubbing Out

No matter how carefully you apply it, a brushed finish seldom looks or feels right when it is cured. There may be small specks of dust and bubbles in the finish, which can be felt when you run your hand across the surface, or slight undulations in the finish, a result of high and low spots that result in an uneven surface. These defects are particularly noticeable on gloss varnishes. Using a satin or an eggshell-sheen varnish as the last top coat can alleviate the

The difference between hand-rubbed gloss (left) and satin (right) is the fineness of the scratches in the finish. Large scratches in the satin sheen diffuse light, resulting in a less glossy finish, as seen in the reflection of the magazine cover.

problem, but neither can provide the look or the silky tactile quality of a hand-rubbed finish.

Rubbing out is a three-step process done with fine abrasives and rubbing compounds. The object is to level imperfections, smooth the finish, and establish a consistent sheen. The sheen can be flat, satin, or gloss, depending on the fineness of the scratch pattern left by the abrasives (the finer the scratches, the glossier the finish).

Although rubbing out levels and smooths the finish, it imparts one final quality that is irresistible. Rubbed-out finishes have a tactile quality that is hard to beat. When finishes feel silky smooth, they just look better. It's almost the same as a car "driving" better when it's clean. It's hard to describe, but when you run your hand along a rubbed satin finish, you'll know what I mean.

Almost all gloss varnishes can be rubbed out to varying degrees of satin and flat, but only certain ones can be rubbed back up to gloss. The best varnishes for rubbing out are phenolic resin/tung oil, sometimes called rubbing varnishes. The varnish must be fully cured, so it's a good idea to wait two weeks or longer before rubbing out. The more the finish is cured, the harder it will be and the better it will rub out. The following techniques can be used on any finish, though they apply primarily to varnish. Nuances and slight differences in technique will be discussed with other finishes in later chapters.

# Rubbing to Satin

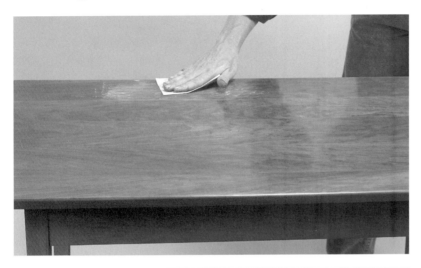

1. Sand out imperfections like small bubbles and dust pimples using 320-grit stearated paper.

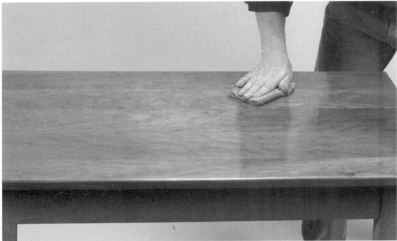

2. Smooth out the finish surface using 0000 steel wool or a gray-grade synthetic abrasive pad.

3. Use 0000 steel wool and a rubbing lubricant to establish a consistent sheen.

## RUBBING TO SATIN OR FLAT

The procedure used for rubbing to satin or flat varies depending on the thickness of the final coat of varnish and the flatness of the surface. If you brushed a thin final coat or used a wiping varnish, there is a danger that you'll rub through the top coat into the coat below it. Because varnish doesn't fuse into the previous coat, this creates a visible outline around the area that you rubbed through (sometimes known as a witness line). If the surface of the wood has slight variations, like hand-planed surfaces or breadboard ends, aggressive rubbing can wear through the high spots of the finish. For these situations, use the following procedure:

To level imperfections like bubbles and dust pimples, sand lightly with 320-grit stearated sandpaper, using your hand as a backing block. Sand all the edges first, using very light pressure.

Next smooth the surface, using 0000 steel wool or a gray-grade synthetic abrasive pad. Rub the finish in long straight strokes, using firm downward pressure. Overlap each stroke slightly until the entire surface shows a dull sheen and there are no shiny spots. This is a flat finish.

To establish a satin sheen, use a pad of 0000 steel wool, soapy water, and a rubbing lubricant like Behlen's Wool-Lube (or paste wax thinned 50/50 with mineral spirits). Rub with the grain in long, firm strokes from one end to the other. Do this at least 20 times, wiping aside the slurry periodically to check your progress. You will see a slight shine start to develop. Let the slurry dry to a haze, buff it off with a soft cloth, and then look at the surface with backlighting. The surface should have an even consistent sheen and look like brushed metal. If there are any shiny spots, they will probably be near the edges. Go back with the dry steel wool and

If the final coat of varnish is thick enough, you can level imperfections with 320- or 400-grit wet/dry paper for a smoother finish.

then the steel wool with the lubricant to touch up these areas. Redo the whole surface several times to blend these areas in.

If the final coat is thick enough, you can vary the procedure just described for a smoother finish. Instead of sanding lightly with the 320-grit stearated sandpaper, use 320-grit wet/dry paper, as shown in the photo on p. 129. (You can start with 400 or 600 grit if there are only minor imperfections in the surface finish.) Wet sanding evens out subtle high and low spots as well as removing any imperfections. Wet-sand through all the grits up to 600 grit. Then switch to a gray-grade synthetic pad and rub the surface until the shiny spots are gone. Finish up with 0000 steel wool, soapy water, and a rubbing lubricant as described on p. 129.

### RUBBING TO GLOSS

Rubbing to gloss, which works best on thick finishes, picks up where the satin leaves off. After wet-sanding with 400 and 600 grits, switch to 800 grit. Then, using 0000 steel wool or a gray-grade synthetic pad with Wool-Lube, rub the entire surface until all the shiny spots are gone. Now switch to a rubbing compound; you can use either 4F pumice mixed with water or a commercial automotive rubbing compound. Follow this step with a finer rubbing compound or rottenstone mixed with water (see the photo below).

How much you need to rub depends on how high a gloss you want. A much faster technique than rubbing by hand is to use a power buffer with automotive rubbing compounds. It's easy to damage the finish with this tool, however, so you may want to practice first. My only advice is to keep the buffer moving at all times. After the final rubbing (by hand or by buffer), apply a glazing compound, which will settle into all the fine scratches and leave a deep, rich gloss.

**To bring up the final gloss, use rottenstone or a fine rubbing compound mixed with a little water.**

# 7

# Lacquers

Lacquer is considered by many to be one of the best all-around finishes for wood. Although not as durable as varnish, it surpasses shellac and most water-based finishes in resistance to heat, moisture, and chemicals. It has exceptional clarity and produces excellent depth and surface luster. Lacquer dries quickly, allowing multiple coats to be applied in one day, and rubbing out can be done after only one or two days' drying time. It rubs out well, fuses to itself between coats, and repairs easily if damaged.

While lacquer has some very attractive advantages, it has another side that poses problems. Lacquer and its vapors are very flammable and toxic. This problem is more of an issue when spraying lacquer, but brushing lacquer requires proper handling and ventilation of vapors, too. An organic-vapor respirator is a must when working in close proximity to the finish, and attention to proper ventilation (see pp. 7-8) is strongly recommended.

## What Is Lacquer?

Like varnish, *lacquer* is an all-encompassing term used to classify a variety of finishing materials. Originally, the term was applied to a type of finish in the Orient that used the natural clear resin from the tree *Rhus vernicifera*. The process of lacquering used as many as

## HOW A SOLVENT-BASED LACQUER DRIES

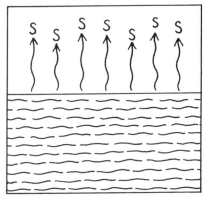

Lacquer is composed of fine, strandlike fluffs of cellulose nitrate dissolved in lacquer thinner. It dries by solvent (S) evaporation.

As the solvent evaporates, the resin strands pack together to form a dried film, which is one-quarter the thickness of the original wet film.

40 applications of the resin tinted with pigments; the colored lacquer was then carved, engraved, or inlaid with gold, silver, or precious stone. It was a highly skilled and arcane process, and there were many attempts to replicate it in the West. The most popular was japanning, introduced in Europe in the 17th century.

Today, lacquer refers to any finishing product that dries primarily by solvent evaporation (see the drawing above). In this sense, lacquers are different from varnishes, which cure by reacting with oxygen in the air through a process called polymerization. (For this reason, lacquers are referred to as solvent-release finishes, while varnishes are called reactive finishes.) Shellac is technically a lacquer, as are the newer water-based formulations of acrylic/polyurethane, which will be discussed in the next chapter.

Lacquers can be made from a variety of resins, but the most common in use for wood finishing today are based on nitrocellulose. Other lacquers use acrylic, vinyl, and cellulose acetate butyrate (CAB); they are similar in composition to nitrocellulose lacquers.

## CHEMICAL COMPOSITION

Most lacquers are formulated to be applied by spraying, but many manufacturers also offer lacquer in brushing formulations. Whether it be a spray lacquer or a brushing lacquer, a typical nitrocellulose lacquer is comprised of four ingredients: resin, modifying resin, plasticizers, and solvent.

The resin used in nitrocellulose lacquer is cellulose nitrate. This synthetic resin is made by reacting pure cellulose with nitric acid and sulfuric acid. (Other applications for this resin are in glue and in inks.) The single most important quality of nitrocellulose is its drying speed; it dries faster than any other resin.

Cellulose nitrate is too brittle to be used as the only resin in a lacquer for wood. Modifying resins are added to the nitrocellulose to make it flexible so that it can accommodate wood movement and adhere well. Many different resins can be added to cellulose nitrate, including shellac, dammar, phenol, and vinyl. The most common resin used today is an alkyd.

Although modifying resins improve flexibility, within a short time the film becomes brittle and will crack or flake off. Special chemicals called plasticizers are added to the lacquer to improve elasticity and to keep the film pliable over time.

The three types of solvents used in a lacquer—active solvents, latent solvents, and diluents—are almost as complex as the resins and plasticizer. Active solvents are true solvents for the lacquer resin; these are ketones (methyl ethyl ketone) and esters (butyl acetate). Latent solvents are not true solvents for the lacquer resin but have the same effect on the resin when used in conjunction with active solvents. Latent solvents are alcohols like ethanol, butanol, and propanol. Diluents are neutral solvents; they have no effect on the resin but "bulk" up the total volume of the thinner to decrease the cost. The most common diluents are toluene and xylene.

# Brushing Lacquer

Since most of the lacquers manufactured today are meant to be sprayed, the options for hand application are limited. However, brushing remains an effective and practical method of application, and brushing lacquers are still widely available for this use. Some manufacturers also make padding lacquers (see p. 139). More finish can be applied with a brush, eliminating much of the labor involved in padding on the finish. In addition, brushing lacquers are more durable than padding lacquers.

## MATERIALS

To brush lacquer correctly requires the appropriate brush as well as the right type of lacquer.

***Brushes*** The best brushes for applying lacquer are those that have a combination of fine, soft bristles and stiffness, namely fitch brushes and very fine, soft China bristle brushes. Synthetic brushes like Chinex also work well. When working with large flat surfaces, you can use a "flow-on" technique to lay down a lot of finish in one application. When using this technique, pick a brush that can hold a lot of finish, like an oval China bristle brush (see the photo below).

***Lacquer*** Lacquers designed for spraying are difficult to brush. While it is possible to add a lacquer retarder to spray lacquers to slow down the drying time, I find it better to use a lacquer designed specifically for brushing. Although many manufacturers are getting away from solvent-based lacquers in favor of the newer water-based lacquers, there's still a wide variety to choose from. Deft-brand brushing lacquer is the most widely available (you can get it from most paint and hardware stores).

If you purchase a brushing lacquer and need to thin it, always use the lacquer thinner specified by the manufacturer. If you use a conventional thinner designed for thinning spray lacquers, it may upset the slow-dry qualities of the brushing lacquer. If the

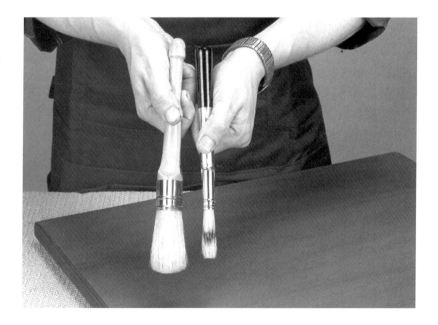

**An oval China bristle brush (left) holds two to three times as much finish as a conventional rectangular fitch brush (right).**

manufacturer does not make a thinner for the lacquer, add lacquer retarder to regular lacquer thinner in the ratio of 1 oz. retarder to 1 qt. thinner. As with any finish, it's always a good idea to strain brushing lacquer before use.

## SEALER COAT

Prepare the wood surface up to at least 180 grit and clean all the dust from the surface. If you want to stain the wood, use a stain that won't pull out with the lacquer solvents; oil/varnish stains, chemical stains, and water-soluble dyes work the best. Let the stain dry overnight. If you want to fill the pores, use a paste wood filler either before or after the first sealer coat (see pp. 65-69).

Sanding sealers are widely available for spray application, but there are none that I know of sold in brushing versions. Thinned lacquer (thinned 50/50) works just as well and also provides the best clarity. You can also use shellac, which is a particularly good idea when refinishing wood to avoid silicone contamination. If you want to use a sanding sealer, you have two options. Use a spraying sanding sealer and work the finish onto the surface quickly; since most of the finish goes into the wood, this usually works fine. Alternatively, you can add lacquer retarder to a spray version to slow down the dry time.

To use thinned lacquer as a sealer, pour some lacquer through a medium-mesh strainer into a clean container and add an equal amount of thinner. Condition the brush in clean lacquer thinner for a minute or so, scrape off the excess thinner, and then dip the brush into the sealer. Start about 3 in. from the edge in the normal manner (see p. 97), and then work the surface from the top to the bottom, overlapping each stroke slightly. Let the sealer dry at least one hour, or longer if the humidity is high. When the sealer is dry, lightly scuff-sand with 320-grit stearated paper to smooth down any raised wood fibers.

## TOP COATS

Wipe the surface of the wood with a clean cloth. Don't worry about removing every last speck of lacquer dust, since the new lacquer will remelt any dust that's still in the pores. Top coats are generally applied full-strength, but if the lacquer seems thick or hard to brush at normal room temperature, thin it with brushing-lacquer thinner. Top coats should be applied in thick coats as evenly as possible, so try to arrange your work so that it lies flat.

**Using a heavily loaded brush, flow the lacquer from one side of the board to the other.**

After conditioning the brush, dip it into strained lacquer about three-quarters the way up the length of the bristle. Leave the brush in the lacquer for several seconds to make sure plenty of finish wicks into the reservoir, and then bring it out of the finish and press the bristles against the side of the can. Start 3 in. from the edge and bring it toward the edge. Immediately come back to where you started and move the brush slowly and deliberately toward the other edge, increasing pressure on the bristle to dispense finish. Try to flow the finish off the brush, as if you're icing a cake. Don't brush it back and forth as though you're painting. The trick is to load the brush with enough finish so that you can make it to the other edge without redipping the brush. If you stop and start in the middle of a brush stroke, you tend to create pools, which can make the finish dry unevenly. Unlike varnish, which can be tipped off after brushing (see pp. 119-120), lacquer can't be rebrushed without wrinkling it and making it worse.

Start the next stroke by overlapping the first one slightly (about ½ in.) and work the surface in the same way from the top to the bottom. Do the edges last. When you're done, the surface will probably look horrible—with brush marks, ridges, and other problems—but resist the temptation to rebrush it! Trying to go back and correct defects only makes them worse. Since lacquer is lower in solids than other finishes like varnish, it will level itself out and dry to a much thinner film than it appears when wet (see the drawing on p. 132). If you leave the surface alone, it should look fine after about an hour or two, when it can be recoated.

You don't have to sand between coats, but if there are wrinkles, pools, or bits of debris, you can sand them level before applying the next coat. Apply as many coats of lacquer as you wish, depending on the effect that you want. If you are going for a rubbed, full-gloss effect, I recommend at least four top coats. Lower-sheen finishes should have at least two or three top coats. Before applying the final coat, I like to level the finish with 320- or 240-grit wet/dry paper, using mineral spirits or soapy water as a lubricant. If you've never wet-sanded a finish before, you may want to dry-sand with stearated paper instead. Dry sanding allows you to see exactly what you're doing, unlike wet sanding, which creates a false illusion of film thickness with the lubricant. After sanding the finish level, wipe the slurry off with a clean rag and apply the final coat.

## Troubleshooting Lacquer Problems

Problems that may arise when applying lacquer by brush include fish-eyes, unevenness of the finish, drips, and blushing.

**Fish-eyes**  Fish-eyes are the result of residual silicone on the wood surface, which causes the lacquer to form small craters resembling fish-eyes around the source of contamination (it's the same problem as with varnish). If fish-eyes appear, wipe the lacquer off the surface immediately. Sealing the wood with shellac instead of lacquer alleviates the problem in most cases, but if fish-eyes still occur, add fish-eye additive to the lacquer before applying it.

**Brush marks, ridges, pools**  If any unevenness results in the dried film, wet-sand it level with 240-grit wet/dry paper before recoating.

**Drips**  If there are drips in the dried film, slice most of the drip off with a sharp chisel, and then wet-sand level with 320-grit paper.

**Blushing**  Blushing is caused by moisture trapped in the wet lacquer, which makes some of the cellulose resin precipitate out of solution. Precipitated cellulose is white, which is why this problem is known as blushing. Blushing occurs only during periods of very high humidity and is easily corrected by applying more lacquer when the relative humidity is lower or by adding a lacquer retarder to the lacquer.

***Alternative top-coat technique***   If you find that the flow-on technique results in excessive brush marks or uneven lacquer thickness, try this alternative top-coat technique. Strain some brushing lacquer into a clean jar or can, and then dilute with an equal amount of thinner. Using a synthetic-bristle artist's brush or a small natural-bristle brush, dip only the first inch or so of the brush into the finish and tap it against the side of the can. You want to load less finish than in the previous technique. Start in from the edges in the normal way (see p. 136), but flow the finish off the brush quickly. Don't worry about trying to reach the other side of the board. Dip the brush into the finish again, and bring it back to where you started, quickly feathering it into the area where you left off, using just the tip of the brush. Work in this brush-and-feather technique until the whole surface is covered. If you miss a spot and can't get to it right away, leave it until the next coat. Do the edges last.

This method of brushing lacquer is suitable for complex surfaces like chairs, moldings, carved areas, and right angles. It is also the best method for applying lacquer to large vertical surfaces where thickly applied lacquer would drip. The brush-and-feather technique deposits less lacquer on the surface since the lacquer is thinned and you're applying a thinner film. Apply two of these top coats to every one of the top coats using the flow-on technique.

**To apply lacquer with the brush-and-feather technique, work small areas with a lightly loaded brush. Flow the lacquer off the brush quickly, and then come back and feather out the brushed area.**

## RUBBING OUT

Of all the finishes discussed in this book, solvent lacquer rubs out the best. This is because of the inherent hardness and brittleness of the nitrocellulose resin, even though it has been modified with other resins to make it more flexible. Also, since the lacquer fuses to itself, there is no chance of rubbing through the last coat and creating a witness line, as with varnish. Most lacquers are cured enough after several days to rub to a satin sheen, and rubbing to gloss can be done after as little as one week's drying time. Of all the advantages of lacquer, its rubbing qualities are what makes it hard to switch to other finishes once you've worked with lacquer.

The procedure for rubbing out lacquer is virtually the same as for rubbing out varnish (see pp. 126-130). The only difference is that you can spend extra time flattening and leveling the film with 320- or 400-grit wet/dry paper. For a satin sheen, stop at 600 grit and finish up with 0000 steel-wool with a rubbing lubricant like Wool-Lube or paste wax as a lubricant. For a gloss finish, continue wet-sanding up to at least 800-grit wet/dry, and then switch to a rubbing compound. On large surfaces, using a power buffer is fast and gives the best results.

## Padding Lacquer

It's possible to wipe on a spray or brushing lacquer with a rag, but as the finish starts to build it becomes tricky to get an even application. To overcome this problem, several manufacturers make padding lacquers, which are formulated so that they can be applied in a manner similar to padding shellac and French polishing (see Chapter 4). A cellulose resin (such as ethyl cellulose or cellulose nitrate) is mixed with shellac, and a small amount of oily solvent (odorless mineral spirits or turpentine) is added so that the pad doesn't stick when applying the finish. The advantage of using this type of oil is that it eventually evaporates, eliminating the need to remove the oil later (the clearing stage in French polishing). The shellac/lacquer/oil ratio varies depending on the manufacturer and the intended use of the products.

Padding lacquers offer durability somewhere between lacquer and shellac. In most cases they have superior heat and alkali resistance, but they can be affected by alcohol the same as shellac. When choosing a padding lacquer to use as a finish, pick one that has a high solids content so it will build reasonably well. Many padding lacquers are formulated as repair mediums; they have low solids content (i.e., more solvent) and in most cases are designed

## HOW LACQUER FUSES TO ITSELF

*When wet lacquer is applied over dried lacquer (top), the solvents redissolve the top of the old lacquer (center) and the result is a fused layer (bottom).*

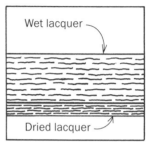

Wet lacquer

Dried lacquer

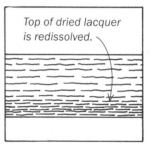

*Top of dried lacquer is redissolved.*

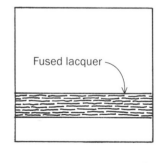

Fused lacquer

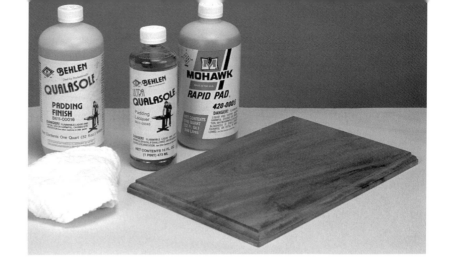

Most padding lacquers are formulated as repair products, but those with a high solids content (shown here) can be used to finish bare wood.

just to remelt the surface of a damaged finish to dissolve scratches and other marks. Of the padding lacquers I've used as complete finishes on bare wood, I prefer Qualasole (made by Behlen, Mohawk), Ultra Qualasole (Behlen), and Rapid Pad (Mohawk).

### APPLYING PADDING LACQUER

Prepare the wood in the same way as for brushing lacquer (see p. 135). Take enough padding-cloth material to fit comfortably in your hand and wet it with about ½ oz. of denatured alcohol to thin the initial lacquer application. Work the alcohol into the cloth, and then make up the pad by folding it so that there are no seams or wrinkles on the bottom. Pour approximately 1 oz. of padding lacquer onto the bottom of the pad.

Starting at the top of the board, wipe the padding lacquer on in stripes, gliding the pad across the surface from one side to the other. Work down the board and do the edges, recharging the pad when it dries out. Keep going over the surface in this striping fashion until a slight shine develops, and then start moving the pad in circles or a figure-eight pattern. When there is an even gloss coating on the board, let the finish dry for at least an hour. Store the pad in an airtight glass jar.

When the finish is dry, lightly scuff-sand the surface with 320-grit stearated sandpaper. Recharge the bottom of the pad, this time using only ½ oz. or less padding lacquer. Using light pressure, move the pad around the surface in a circular pattern. Vary the size of the circle so that all areas of the board are covered. The oil in the lacquer will keep the pad from sticking as long as you keep it moving. Recharge the pad only when it's dry and stop when the finish has built up to a discernible thickness. Let the lacquer dry overnight.

After wetting the padding cloth with denatured alcohol, dispense the padding lacquer onto the bottom of the pad.

Work down the board from top to bottom, wiping the lacquer on in stripes.

Continue the above process until the finish is built up to your liking, but don't apply too much lacquer in one application. Thinner coats with proper drying in between build and dry better than one or two thick coats. When the finish is dry you have two options, depending on whether you want a satin finish or a gloss finish.

*Satin finish*   If you want a satin finish, allow the finish to dry for several days. Then use some 0000 steel wool to rub a mixture of wax thinned 50/50 with mineral spirits over the finish. Rub in long strokes with the grain. When the wax hazes over, buff it up to a satin sheen with a clean, dry cloth. You can apply a second application of wax with a cloth pad after waiting a day.

If the finish has ridges left from the padding process or bits of debris stuck in it, level the finish first by sanding lightly with 400-grit stearated sandpaper.

**Gloss finish**   If you prefer a gloss finish, make up a fresh pad and dampen it with ½ oz. of denatured alcohol. Pour ½ oz. of padding lacquer on the bottom of the pad and tap it against your palm to disperse it into the center of the pad. The pad should feel moist, but not wet. Squeeze the pad hard to wring out any excess lacquer. Bring the pad down lightly on the surface and move it in a circular pattern, covering the board evenly. Always keep the pad moving, not letting it rest even for a second. As the pad dries out, increase the pressure by using both hands. Don't worry if the dry pad leaves marks on the surface at first—the marks will disappear as you increase pressure with the pad and burnish a gloss onto the surface of the lacquer. Finish up by "buffing" with the dry pad, moving it rapidly back and forth with the grain of the wood.

**To prepare to buff to a gloss finish, tap the pad against the palm of your hand to disperse the lacquer evenly into the center of the pad.**

**Buff the surface of the finish to gloss by moving the pad briskly back and forth.**

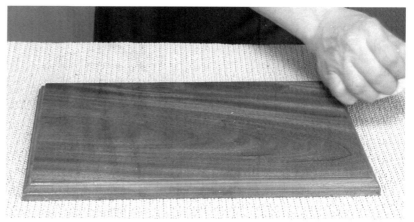

# 8

# Water-Based Finishes

The emergence of water-based finishes in the last decade or so has been in response to the hazards associated with conventional solvent-based lacquers. The solvents used to dissolve the lacquer resins and to thin the material for spraying are flammable and toxic to humans, but these hazards are only part of the problem. The vapors from spraying lacquer contribute to poor air quality, and many states have passed strict laws that limit the amount of VOCs (volatile organic compounds) that companies can exhaust into the air. While many companies continue to use solvent-based finishes by converting to different methods of spraying, using finishes with lower VOCs, and scrubbing the exhaust, some experts feel that it is only a matter of time before water-based lacquer becomes the standard finish for factory-produced furniture.

When you apply a finish by wiping it or brushing it, you circumvent some of the hazards associated with solvent finishes. However, health hazards, objectionable odors, and storage and disposal of solvent-based products are still problems. For many finishers, switching to water-based finishes becomes a good alternative. There's only one problem. Water-based finishes are very different products from solvent finishes. They look different when dry, handle differently, and require controlled application. For finishers used to the aesthetic and handling qualities of solvent finishes, water-based finishes take some getting used to.

Like any other finishing product for wood, water-based finishes have some distinct advantages and disadvantages. The advantages are nonflammability, a less-polluting solvent vapor, a high solids content (meaning that finishes build fast), easy cleanup, fast drying time, and nonyellowing. Disadvantages include weather-sensitivity in application, grain-raising, and sensitivity to storage (some products have a usable shelf life and become unusable if frozen). Another issue is aesthetics. Most water-based finishes are optically neutral or slightly bluish and do not add the characteristic warmth to wood that we associate with traditional finishes like oils, lacquer, and shellac. On some woods, like walnut and mahogany, this trait is very noticeable and not particularly pleasing. On the other hand, this characteristic can be an advantage, as with white or pickled finishes, which would appear yellow or amber if you used a solvent varnish or lacquer.

## What Is a Water-Based Finish?

The majority of water-based finishes are, by definition, lacquers because they dry by solvent evaporation. Like any other lacquer, they are composed of resins and solvents. But most of the harmful and polluting solvents have been replaced by water, which is normally not a compatible solvent for any of the resins. To get water to become compatible with the resins, other chemicals are added to create an emulsion, a chemical term for a mixture of two substances that normally do not mix with each other. The chemicals ensure that the resin is evenly dispersed in the liquid carrier.

### CHEMICAL COMPOSITION

Resins used in water-based finishes include acrylic, modified acrylics, and urethane. Acrylic and modified acrylics are clear, hard, and brittle (like Plexiglas) and contribute nonyellowing clarity with good rubbing qualities. Urethane is tough and contributes scratch, solvent, and heat resistance. Urethane is usually modified with varying amounts of acrylic or can be a modified urethane/oil-type resin similar to those used in oil-based varnishes.

# How a Water-Based Finish Dries

If you could enlarge a small amount of water-based finish, you would see that tiny droplets of resin and solvent (glycol ether) are dispersed within the water (carrier). This dispersion, known as an emulsion, accounts for the milky appearance of the finishing material. (Milk is an emulsion of water and butterfat.)

When a water-based finish is applied to the wood, the water evaporates, forcing the droplets of resin/solvent together. The solvent keeps the resin sticky enough so that the droplets fuse together. When the solvent evaporates, the resin droplets dry to a smooth, clear, contiguous film.

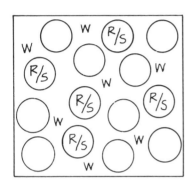

Resin/solvent droplets are dispersed in water.

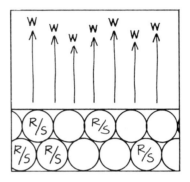

The water evaporates, compressing the resin/solvent droplets.

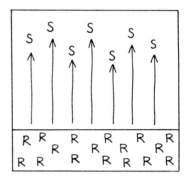

When the solvent evaporates, the resin coalesces into a smooth, contiguous film.

For application of the finish, a liquid is needed to disperse the resin. In solvent-based lacquers, the carrier would be a solvent that dissolves or is at least compatible with the resin. Water is the carrier used in water-based lacquers; it is what makes these products less hazardous and nonflammable.

Chemicals called surfactants keep the noncompatible resins and water in a homogenous emulsion and improve the flowout of the finish (they keep the water from beading up when the finish is applied). Surfactants are similar to soaps and create bubbles when the lacquer is applied. Defoamers are added to minimize the formation of bubbles.

Some type of solvent is necessary to keep the dispersed resin sticky enough so that it can eventually form a contiguous film (see the sidebar on p. 145). Glycol ethers are used because they are both resin- and water-compatible.

Besides the above ingredients, other chemicals may be added to improve flowout and leveling for certain applications and to improve product stability. In addition, flatteners may be added to reduce sheen.

### CHARACTERISTICS OF WATER-BASED FINISHES

Although water-based products all look similar when they're in the can, don't expect them to handle, look, and protect the same once they're on the wood. The resins used in making water-based finishes have slight color differences, which affect how the finish looks on the wood. Acrylics are optically neutral and do not alter the natural color of wood one way or another. When applied to wood, they make it look very close to the same color as it is in its dry state. Modified acrylics are warmer in color. Urethanes can have a bluish tint, which makes naturally warm woods like walnut and mahogany look very cold. The blue tint counteracts the orange tint in the wood (see p. 53). An exception is the modified urethane/oil water-based finishes, which have the characteristic warmth and depth of the solvent-based equivalents. As discussed previously, the resins also determine the durability of the finish.

The rest of the components—solvent, surfactants, and defoamers—all determine how the finish will handle. Brushes and

## Choosing a Water-Based Finish

As with other finishing products, you may be confused when you go to the store to purchase a water-based finish. Some products readily identify the resins with such names as water-based urethane or acrylic lacquer. Others use names like polycrylic to denote mixtures of the two. If the name doesn't identify the resin(s), look on the back of the can and see whether it lists the ingredients.

Manufacturers don't generally disclose the exact type of ingredients used in their formulations, so you might want to try several brands and experiment on test pieces. Of the brands I've used over the years I like the brushing qualities of CrystaLac brushing lacquer and General Finishes' Polyurethane and Acrylic Blend. These two finishes are neutral in color. For a bit more warmth, try Waterlox Waterworks II. This is an oil/urethane formulation that flows out extremely well off the brush and has some of the warmth and depth of a solvent-based urethane.

applicator pads tend to create bubbles, and if the correct amount of defoamer is not present, you'll have problems. The solvents in the formulation determine the drying time of the finish and flowout and leveling. Surfactants also have an effect on flowout of the finish.

## General Guidelines for Using Water-Based Finishes

The type of preparation you do and the materials you use are particularly important when working with water-based finishes. Materials that are commonly used with other finishes cannot be used or must be used differently. Follow these guidelines regardless of whether you are applying the finish by brush or by pad.

### PREPARING THE SURFACE

In most cases, you need to preraise the grain before you apply a water-based finish to bare wood. Prepare the surface of the wood to at least 180 grit and clean off all residue. Using a clean rag or sponge, wet the wood with distilled water and let it dry for several hours. Then sand the wood with 220 grit to knock down the raised grain.

There are two instances where it's not necessary to raise the grain. The first is if you use a sealer coat of shellac; the shellac won't raise the grain as much as a water-based sealer coat, and it will prevent the water-based top coat from raising the grain. The second is if you use an oil/varnish-based stain; the stain will seal the surface of the wood and prevent the water-based sealer from raising the grain.

### COLORING AND FILLING THE WOOD

Some colorants pull up into the water-based finish as you apply the finish. The worst offenders are dye stains, which are redissolved by the water and/or solvents in the finish. I recommend that you seal all dyes with a shellac sealer before applying water-based top coats (see the photo on p. 148). Oil/varnish stains are the best as long as they are fully cured (allow two days). Check with the manufacturer of the finish to see if there is an adhesion problem; if in doubt, seal the oil/varnish stain with dewaxed shellac to minimize adhesion problems. Many manufacturers also make pigmented stains and dye stains that are 100% compatible with their products.

The best glazes to use between coats of water-based finishes are thinned UTCs (universal tinting colors) or water-based stains, both dye-type and pigment (don't use oil-based glazes). The gel versions of these stains work best. All of these glazes "bite" into, or slightly

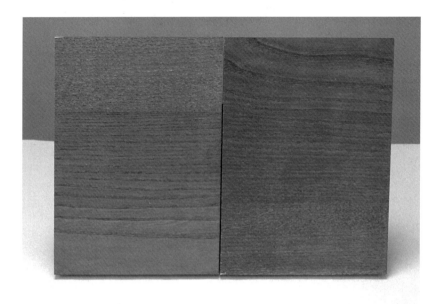

Applying a water-based finish over a dye stain can pull out the color from the board (left). Sealing the dye with shellac first helps hold the color (right).

dissolve, the finish, so be sure to practice on scraps to get a feel for how they handle. The glazes cannot be removed completely if you don't like the color.

Any paste-wood filler can be used under a water-based finish. Water-based fillers are the best in terms of compatibility, but oil-based fillers work fine as long as they are fully dry and you seal them with a coat of shellac before applying the water-based top coats.

### SEALING THE WOOD

Water-based finishes are self-sealing, which means that you don't have to use a special sealer with them and they don't need to be thinned. Shellac also makes a good sealer for water-based finishes because it doesn't raise the grain, but you should use only a dewaxed shellac to avoid possible adhesion problems. The shellac's color also warms up woods that would normally look washed out with neutral or bluish water-based top coats.

### SANDING BETWEEN COATS

You can use most types of sandpaper to sand between coats, as long as you remove the residue completely before applying more finish. I discourage the use of stearated sandpaper because it can leave trace amounts of zinc-stearate lubricant on the surface, which can cause problems if not completely removed. Steel wool should never be used because tiny shreds may come off and cause spotting with subsequent finishing coats; use synthetic abrasive pads instead

Always strain a water-based finish before you use it to remove any bits of dried finish.

(see p. 31). To remove all sanding residue, wipe the surface with water or a water-based glass cleaner and a clean rag or paper towel. Glass cleaners have many of the same chemicals that are used in the formulation of the water-based finishes and won't interfere with application of the finish.

### STRAINING THE FINISH

Water-based finishes do not redissolve in their original solvent when dry. Small bits of dried finish may fall back into the finish from around the edge of the can when it's reopened. These should be removed by straining the finish through a medium-mesh paint strainer. Using a hammer and nail set, punch holes through the lip of the can so that you don't get a buildup of finish in the lip.

## Brushing Water-Based Finishes

The technique for brushing water-based finish is similar to that used for brushing solvent lacquer (see pp. 135-138), with one major difference. While most solvent lacquers brush the same, there is a big difference in the brushing quality of water-based products. Some of them foam excessively, others do not flow out well and show brush marks, and others take a long time to dry. The reason for this variability in performance lies in the formulation of each of the finishes. The balance of ingredients in a water-based finish is

Punch holes around the lip of the can to allow the finish to drain back into the can.

very delicate, and the addition of too much of one ingredient to correct one problem may upset other factors. Most problems can be corrected by applying thinner coats and/or by using a different brush. If you continue to have problems, you may want to use a retarder additive supplied by the manufacturer or switch to a different product.

The best brushes to use with water-based finishes are 100% synthetic filament. I like Chinex, a Dupont filament that is very fine and soft. Synthetic-bristle artist's brushes made with Taklon are also very good brushes; their small size makes them well suited to cutting in, detail work, and small projects. Avoid cheap brushes that have thick filaments with blunt ends. These brushes will always leave brush marks.

### FIRST COAT

Begin by arranging backlighting to highlight any spots that you may miss on the surface. Condition your brush in the normal manner (see p. 11), and then dip the brush halfway up the bristles into some strained finish. As with most brushing situations, start a few inches in from one edge and brush the finish toward that edge. Come back to where you started and brush in the opposite direction, toward the other edge (see the photo below). Try to flow the finish off the brush slowly. Using the tip of the brush, very lightly smooth out any irregularities like pools and bubbles as you work (see the photo on the facing page). Continue down the surface, overlapping each stroke slightly. Although the surface may look uneven, avoid the temptation to overwork the finish with the brush. Water-based finishes should level themselves if you apply enough finish and leave them alone.

**Flow the finish off the brush slowly as you work from one edge of the board to the other.**

**Work out bubbles and other imperfections with the very tip of the brush.**

## TOP COATS

You can recoat with a second coat of finish once the first coat is dry. Since water-based finishes vary in dry times, refer to the manufacturer's instructions. When the humidity is high, you may have to wait longer; wait until the finish feels dry when you rub your hand on it. If the surface has large bits of debris, bubbles, or brush marks, you should wait until the finish is hard enough to wet-sand (it shouldn't gum). I use 320- or 240-grit wet/dry paper with water as a lubricant. (Don't use soapy water because it could cause adhesion problems with the next coat.) Follow with a maroon-grade synthetic pad. Wipe off the slurry with water or glass cleaner and a lint-free cloth. Make sure you remove all the dried finish since the new finish will not redissolve the sanding dust.

Water-based finishes have a high solids content, so you can get a very durable finish with only three applications. Apply one or two more coats if you're rubbing the finish to gloss (see p. 154).

If excessive foaming is a problem when applying the finish, try loading the brush with less finish and brushing on a thinner coat. When you've brushed the entire surface, wipe all the finish off the brush and come back and quickly "tip off" the finish (see p. 119). Thinner coats dry more quickly, so you'll be able to apply them without waiting a long time between coats. Applying thinner coats takes a little more work, but the finish will be easier to rub out later because it will dry harder more quickly. Using a different brush can also help with finishes that are prone to bubbling. Some synthetic brushes have flags manufactured on the bristle ends that may cause tiny bubbles to form. Switching to a tapered, nonflagged brush (see the drawing on p. 11) should help alleviate this problem.

When applying water-based finish with an applicator pad, first scrape the excess finish off the pad.

Use enough pressure on the pad to dispense the finish evenly.

## Applying Water-Based Finishes with a Pad

Applicator pads hold a lot of finish and are useful when you have a large surface to do. Using a pad doesn't leave as fine a finish as good brushwork, but proper rubbing out will level most surface irregularities.

To use an applicator pad, strain some finish into a paint roller tray or other large, shallow pan. Set the applicator pad into the finish and let it sit for half a minute, and then scrape the excess finish off the pad by pulling it along the top edge of the pan, as shown in the photo at left above. Swipe the pad from one end of the board to the other, using enough pressure to dispense finish evenly on the surface (see the photo at right above). Come back with a lighter touch to remove bubbles and smooth out the finish (see the photo on the facing page). Then apply another swipe, overlapping the first application by only ½ in. or so. Repeat until you have an even coating of finish on the entire surface.

Pads leave noticeable ridges in the wet finish, but try to ignore them: If you've applied a thick enough coat, the weight of the finish will level them out. If there is excessive bubbling, you are using too much pressure on the pad. Localized bubbling, as along the edges, can be smoothed out with a dry brush. Any drips along the edges can be evened out afterwards with a small brush.

Go back over the surface with a lighter touch to smooth out any bubbles or other imperfections.

## Adjusting the Color of Water-Based Finishes

Water-based finishes do not add the characteristic warmth that you get with most other finishes. They also do not penetrate, which is what adds the deepening effect and grain enhancement of finishes like oils. In some cases, as with pickled finishes, these are effects you may be avoiding. In other cases, you may want to get a water-based finish to look like a solvent finish. There are several ways to do this.

The most foolproof method I've found for adjusting the color is to apply a thin glaze of UTCs (universal tinting colors) or water-based stains after the first coat of finish is dry. Use burnt sienna or any other combination to get an orangish brown. Dilute the color with water and apply it to the surface, and then wipe it off until you get the intensity of color that you want. Let the glaze dry several hours before brushing on another coat of water-based finish.

Another way to adjust the color is to use a dye to stain the wood before applying the finish. If you stain the wood with a very dilute amber/yellow dye, it will highlight the grain and warm up the wood (see the sidebar on pp. 54-55).

A third way to adjust the color of a water-based top coat is to add a dye to the finish. For example, adding an amber dye creates a warmer look but will not accentuate the wood grain as much as using a dye first. Don't put the dry powder directly in the finish

## Cleaning Up Water-Based Finishes

Although water-based finishes clean up easily with soap and water, there are a couple of precautions to follow. Try to clean all tools immediately after use. After a water-based finish has dried or partially dried, it will not clean easily. When I'm applying several coats over a short period, I keep the brush (or pad) soaking in water, then spin (or blot) out the excess before the next coat.

Clean all tools in warm water and soap. Don't use hot water because it may cause the finish to gel slightly, actually making cleanup more difficult. If your brush has dried with water-based finish in it, you may be able to rescue the brush by soaking it in furniture stripper (see p. 13).

since it won't dissolve properly. Instead, dissolve a very small amount of dye in some water and then add it to the finish. Since all dyes vary in concentration it's hard to give precise instructions, but start with a thimbleful of dye in 1 oz. of water. Add a little of this base to a pint of finish and, after stirring, check the color by wiping some of the finish on some white bond paper. Very little dye is needed to adjust the color of the finish, so take it easy. Always use dilute strengths of dye or you'll get visible lap marks when you brush it.

You can also use premixed NGR (non-grain-raising) dye stains to adjust the color. Use a thimbleful of dye per pint as above. Many companies also sell "amber-additives," which are dyes predissolved in a solvent compatible with the water-based finish.

## Rubbing Out Water-Based Finishes

Rubbing out a water-based finish is similar to rubbing out any other finish (see pp. 126-130), but there are a couple of problems that you may encounter. The first is the problem of witness lines. Some water-based finishes will not fuse, or "burn in," between coats, and witness lines may be visible when you rub through the top coat. To get around this problem, I recommend the following technique: Rather than applying one heavy final coat, apply three thinner coats, waiting until the finish is dry to the touch but still soft before recoating. Before applying the final coat, wet-sand the surface level with 220-grit wet/dry paper and remove the slurry with a lint-free cloth (I use Kimwipes, a product sold by laboratory supply companies to clean glassware). Use your best brushwork so the finish will need very little leveling when rubbing out. I wait at least a week before rubbing out; the longer you wait, the better the finish will rub out.

The second problem you are likely to encounter is in rubbing to gloss. As with solvent varnishes, some water-based finishes rub out to gloss better than others. Acrylic contributes good rubbing qualities, so look for this in the formulation if you intend to rub to gloss. Urethanes will not rub to gloss evenly. Another problem in rubbing to gloss is that many rubbing and polishing compounds in paste form contain solvents that will soften water-based finishes. This shows up as a haze on the gloss finish. I use Meguiar's rubbing compounds (available at most auto-supply stores) for rubbing to gloss on water-based finishes. After leveling and wet-sanding to 800 grit, begin with #1, followed by #2, and then finally #10 Plastic Polish. This sequence will not produce any haze.

# 9

# Milk Paint

Commercially prepared paint was not available in this country until the early 1800s. Before that time, people made their own paint to apply to their own hand-made furniture, using formulas passed down from generation to generation. One such paint, known as milk paint, was prepared from milk, quicklime, and dry earth colors. This paint has proved extremely durable, and many pieces of furniture hundreds of years old still exist today with the original paint intact.

## What Is Milk Paint?

Milk paint gets its name from the chemical binder that adheres the pigment to the surface of the wood. The principal protein in milk is casein—the solids in milk that form the curds to make cheese. These curds are produced by adding acid (vinegar) to skim milk, and the precipitated curds are washed to separate the whey. When the curds are dried they form casein, which has been used for centuries as a strong glue. Casein is insoluble in water—it must be mixed with an alkali like quicklime, which produces a thin colloidal suspension. This mixture is the perfect medium for adding dry colors to make a paint. (Painting with a glue binder, whether milk or animal glue, is called distemper.) The colors available to our early ancestors were the natural colors found in the earth around

This milk-painted Windsor chair has a lot of interesting surfaces for creating antique effects, as seen on the carved knuckles of the arm and on the edges of the seat.

them. The earth pigment colors are subdued, which accounts for the muted colors characteristic of milk paint. In addition to the pigments, chalk and clay were added to act as fillers or extenders to increase the covering power of the pigments.

Milk paint has a dual personality. Left "off the brush" it has a rough, unsophisticated look that adds charm to plain, utilitarian objects. Smoothed out and finished with an oil or other clear finish, it adds an air of elegance to a graceful piece like a Windsor chair. Milk paint is also a great finish for producing antique and distressed effects (see the photo at left).

## Brushing Milk Paint

Brushing is the only way to apply milk paint by hand. Because it is water based, milk paint dries quickly and several coats can be applied in one day.

### MATERIALS
Although it's possible to make your own milk paint (see the sidebar on the facing page), modern versions are available, either in a premixed liquid form similar to latex paint or in a dry powder. I find the dry version more authentic looking; it is available in assorted colors from The Old Fashioned Milk Paint Company (436 Main Street, Groton, MA 01450-0222; 508-448-6336) and uses the same ingredients as the original formulas. The paint is mixed with water, stirred thoroughly, and then applied to the wood. Because the carrier is water, the paint is nonflammable, and there are no fumes or unpleasant odors to worry about. The downsides to milk paint are minor. First, the lime makes the paint caustic, so you must wash it off your skin immediately (I recommend you wear gloves when you mix it). Second, once milk paint is mixed you have to use it within a couple of days. After that time the paint loses some of its natural properties and has to be discarded.

Since milk paint uses water as the carrier, synthetic-bristle brushes work best. For large areas, I recommend a 2-in. Chinex brush; for precise control in tight areas, use a synthetic-bristle artist's brush with a square edge like Taklon.

### PREPARING THE SURFACE
The surface to be painted should be clean, dry, and sanded to at least 120 grit. Hand planes and other edge tools like scrapers make an excellent surface treatment because the texture from hand tools shows under the thin milk paint. Milk paint doesn't need a primer or

# Making Your Own Milk Paint

Making milk paint is economical and can be fun as well. The recipe at right is adapted from *Formulas for Painters* by Robert Massey (Watson-Guptill Publications, New York, 1967). The amounts are listed as parts/volume; if you use ounces as a reference, the recipe will make about 1½ pints. The ingredients can be purchased through various suppliers. Lime is available from hardware stores and garden centers. Casein and dry pigments can be purchased from art-supply stores and some specialty finishing suppliers. (Use only lime-proof dry pigments.) If you have problems finding these materials in your area, try the Johnson Paint Company, 355 Newbury Street, Boston, MA 02115; (617) 536-4244.

## Ingredients

| | |
|---|---|
| Powdered casein | 2 parts/volume |
| Water | 15 parts/volume |
| Lime | 2 parts/volume |
| Dry pigments | 8 parts/volume |
| Whiting (calcium carbonate) | 8 parts/volume |

Sift the casein slowly into half of the water, stirring to get rid of lumps. When the mixture is smooth, add the lime and stir, let stand for 30 minutes, and then stir in the remaining water.

Mix the dry pigments and whiting together and add slowly to the casein solution, stirring constantly.

The proportions given above yield a one-coat-coverage milk paint about the consistency of cream, but more water can be added to suit your needs. You can also adjust the ratio of whiting to dry pigments. More whiting gives a more translucent, chalky color, while more pigment will produce a more opaque effect.

special sealer on new wood, but it is advisable to raise the grain with water. On previously painted wood you should clean the surface with mineral spirits and coarse steel wool and then scuff-sand with 120-grit sandpaper. If the piece was stripped, I recommend that you seal the surface with a primer coat of pigmented shellac (BIN, sold by Zinsser, is a good product). After the primer is dry, scuff-sand with 150-grit sandpaper.

## APPLYING MILK PAINT

You can use milk paint two ways. When the powder is mixed with an equal amount of water, it easily covers up the wood surface with one or two coats. Mixed with double the amount of water, it can be used as a stain or wash, which lets some of the grain and figure of the wood come through (see the top photo on p. 158). Experiment on scraps to see which effect you prefer.

**Mixed at normal consistency, one coat of milk paint almost completely covers up the grain (left). Diluted, milk paint lets the grain of the pine show through (right).**

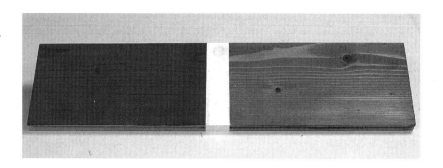

**Using a synthetic-bristle brush, apply the first coat evenly, overlapping the strokes slightly.**

Although it is possible to get single-coat coverage, I prefer to apply two thinner coats of milk paint. You should experiment to get the right consistency, but if you use the paint from Old Fashioned Milk Paint Co., it should be slightly thinner than the consistency of cream. I mix the milk paint in a two-cup plastic container, which is easy to clean when you're done painting. Be sure to stir the paint thoroughly, and keep stirring throughout the painting process since some of the pigment will settle to the bottom. The paint will start to thicken in use, but you can always add more water to restore the correct brushing consistency. Brush on the first coat evenly, overlapping the strokes slightly. Don't worry if some of the paint looks splotchy as it dries—the next coat will take care of these areas.

Although the paint appears to dry rapidly, let it sit at least four hours and then scuff-sand with 320-grit stearated paper. You'll see a lot of paint powder come off with this step and you might get a rub-through, but, again, the next coat of paint will cover any problems. When you've finished sanding, dust the piece off thoroughly and then wipe it down with a damp rag. Apply the second coat of paint just like the first, being careful to get even coverage.

Allow the paint to dry overnight. Now you have two choices: You can leave the paint as is, which is dry and chalky, or you can apply a top coat of clear finish to deepen the color and change the tactile quality of the paint. For objects that may be around water, I strongly suggest using some type of top coat since untreated milk paint water-spots easily. For outdoor projects, a coat of spar alkyd varnish or polyurethane is needed. As a rule, oil-based products deepen the color of the paint significantly, while water-based lacquers and clear wax deepen it less (see the top photo on the facing page).

If you simply want to smooth the surface but keep the dry look, rub the paint with 0000 steel wool. A light coat of clear paste wax will add some smoothness to the finish.

Varnish (right) deepens milk paint the most, while water-based lacquer (left) deepens the color less. The center section is untreated.

## Special Effects

Milk paint lends itself to a variety of creative effects, especially those used to simulate the look of old furniture. Distressing, crackle, flaking, and chipping are all easily done with milk paint.

### DISTRESSING

Many finishers like to "distress" painted furniture to give it an appearance of age. Distressing involves rubbing through sharp edges near areas that would be exposed to natural wear and tear such as drawers, door edges, and knobs. Some finishers really attack the piece with nails, files, chains, and so forth, but I prefer more subtle effects. My favorite technique is simply to rub through edges with 100-grit sandpaper or a piece of rope, as shown in the photo at right. (The rope also burnishes the surface as it wears through, creating a more convincing effect.) Carved and raised areas like the knuckle on a Windsor chair and the edges of the seat are good areas to distress (see the photo on p. 156). Do the distressing after the last coat of paint and before applying the clear top coat. Go right through to the wood. Dye the bare wood with a dilute yellow/amber-colored water-soluble dye to simulate patina. You can also apply a dark glaze over the paint in corners and other recessed areas.

To avoid an overdone look when distressing, try to think of the points of wear that a piece of furniture is likely to receive. Proceed slowly and resist the temptation to do too much distressing at one time. Also, don't do symmetrical distressing. For example, the two arms of a chair get different types of wear, depending on whether the person using it is right-handed or left-handed. Refer to the drawing on p. 160 for help in locating areas to distress.

Use a piece of thick rope to rub through the edges.

# POINTS OF WEAR

Burnishing rub-throughs where head rubs

Rub-throughs on tops of arms and knuckles

Burnishing rub-throughs on front of spindles and arm spindles

Chips, crackle where paint pools around spindles

Rub-throughs on front edges of seat and medial stretcher

Chips, flakes on front of legs

Crackle, dents, gouges on top surface

Rub-throughs, rounding on edges and sharp corners

Rub-throughs on top of drawer, on knob, and on front, sides, and backs of legs

Rub-throughs on edges of legs (toward bottom only)

Rub-throughs on sharp corners of molding, inside door edges, and front edges of shelf

Rub-throughs, burnishing, crackle on knob

Rub-throughs, dents around knob

Dents, gouges on shelves

Rub-throughs on bottom of door

A more aged look can be achieved by applying two contrasting colors of milk paint and then sanding through the last color to expose the first coat underneath (see the photo at right). But be careful with this technique because the effect can look contrived if not done subtly. Try to use two very different colors, like dark green over white, black over red, or white over black. Make sure the top-coat color is dry before sanding. (I recommend you wait several days; otherwise, the top coat tends to gum up and tear when you sand it.)

## CRACKLE

Over time, oil-based paints and clear finishes lose their elasticity and are no longer able to withstand the seasonal expansion and contraction of wood. When this happens, the finish will crack or craze into a criss-cross series of lines. When this crazing is an authentic part of an antique piece of furniture or painting it is referred to as *craquelure*. When done deliberately for special effects or to simulate age on a new piece of furniture, it is called *crackle*.

There are a variety of crackle effects you can reproduce using different mediums. Special crackle mediums are available, but the simplest one to use is hide glue, either premixed or made from dry granules (hot hide glue). The glue works only with water-based paints, and the effects you can reproduce are endless.

For the best effect, use a contrasting color under the layer of paint that you crack. Brush on a coat of latex or milk paint for the ground coat. I use latex paint tinted to the color I want because it's much cheaper than milk paint. The aesthetic and tactile difference of the latex paint isn't all that noticeable because there isn't a lot of it exposed. Let the ground coat dry fully (waiting 24 hours is best). Next, using hide glue thinned to brushing consistency (usually one part glue to one part water), brush a coat of glue evenly over the surface you intend to crackle. Let it dry at least several hours and then apply another coat of glue. If the dried glue is rough, smooth it with 120-grit sandpaper. Brush on an even coat of the crackle layer of paint. As the paint starts to dry it will crack apart, but you can hasten the process by using a hair dryer or a heat gun set on low.

There are several ways to control the size of the crack pattern. By varying the thickness and location of the glue you can create fine crackle (thin glue areas) to large cracks (thick glue areas). Deliberately overheating areas with the heat gun also produces larger, flaking-type cracks. By selectively applying glue in certain areas and not others, you can choose which areas you want to produce cracks.

**Applying two different-colored paints and then sanding through the top color produces an interesting antique effect.**

**Glue was applied heavily on the scooped area of the seat to produce large cracks.**

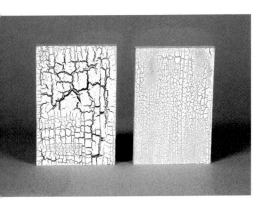

**Varying the thickness of the paint over a coat of hide glue allows you to control the size of the crack pattern.**

You can also control the type of cracks you get by brushing on thinner or thicker coats of paint over the glue. Thin coats of paint create small, hairline cracks, while thick coats produce larger, wider cracks (see the photo at left).

If you've never tried crackle before, I suggest you use premixed hide glue. It's easier to handle than hot hide glue. Beyond this advice, you're on your own. Experiment on lots of scraps and be sure to write down exactly what you do in what order so that you can duplicate it later. My own preference is for restraint with crackle. I like the finer, lighter crackle pattern, or crackle confined to areas where the original paint may have pooled, as at the base of spindles. Large wide cracks over an entire piece of furniture can look contrived. You can top-coat the cracked layer of paint with a clear-finish top coat if you want. As explained previously, different finishes produce darker, deeper effects.

If you can't get the top layer to crackle, it's because there isn't enough glue underneath, either because the glue has been overthinned or is being absorbed into the first coat of paint. Experimenting on scraps first will help you determine the right amount of glue to use.

### FLAKING

When moisture gets underneath paint, it causes the paint to flake off; prolonged exposure to the sun or heat will also produce flaking. You can mimic this effect and create a very convincing antique look

**For a flaked effect, apply paint over paste wax and rub off the dry paint with your thumb.**

by applying paste wax to selected areas of a piece of furniture with a coarse-bristle brush before brushing on the top coat of paint. The paint will tend to bead up when applied over the wax, so you may have to double-coat it to get even coverage. When the paint is dry, flake it off with a piece of steel wool or your thumb (see the bottom photo on the facing page). Be sure to remove the wax residue with some naphtha if you're applying a finish over the paint.

## CHIPPING

Chips can be created exactly where you want them by heating the paint with a heat gun. Milk paint will blister only when applied over glue or when the paint is thick enough and not fully dry. Oil paints and partially dried latex will blister without glue. As with other distressing effects, chips look best when there is a contrasting color underneath.

Using a heat gun set on high, hold the gun about an inch or two away from the paint where you want it to chip. Sharp edges, corners, and places where paint may have pooled are good locations for chipped areas. When the paint starts to bubble, remove the gun and wait several minutes for the paint to cool. Then scrape the blistered paint off with a knife, a scraper, or any sharp tool. You can burnish the area with steel wool or sandpaper to smooth out the sharp edges of the chip.

## BURNISHING

Burnishing is a process used to simulate the natural polishing of a paint by repeated contact with hands and clothing. To duplicate this look, use a cotton rag to buff the area shoe-shine style with moderate pressure, as shown in the photo at right. Try to confine this treatment to milk paint that hasn't been top-coated with finish. The burnished areas provide a nice contrast to the dry chalky areas of the rest of the paint.

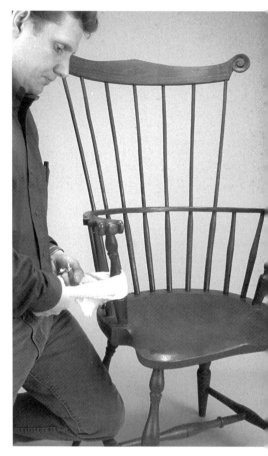

**To burnish dry paint, buff it shoe-shine style with a rag.**

# 10

# Maintaining and Repairing Finishes

In spite of manufacturers' claims to the contrary, there are no finishes for wood that are completely impervious to abuse. All surface finishes need routine maintenance in the form of cleaning and polishing, and in time they may need some type of repair to scratches, dents, and damage from water and other solvents. Caring for furniture involves protecting it from environmental factors, maintaining the appearance with waxes and polishes, cleaning the surface to remove the buildup of dirt and grime, and making major surface and finish repairs.

## Protecting Finishes from Sunlight and Humidity

Over time, all surface finishes react with the surrounding environment and become dull or fade and eventually may crack, chip, or peel off the wood. In most cases this process is a gradual one, and it may take many years to notice any appreciable change in appearance (the change may go unnoticed until the object is moved to a location where the lighting is different). This deterioration is brought about by many factors, but the ones within your control are sunlight and relative humidity.

Prolonged exposure to direct sunlight causes fading of stains and yellowing of surface films. The heat produced by strong sunlight will degrade finishes (as can occur when an object is placed in front of a southern window) and in extreme cases can crack and split wood. Relative humidity is a more insidious problem because it is harder to control. Rapid fluctuations in relative humidity cause abrupt changes in dimension across the grain of the wood, which can result in crazing and checking of surface finishes as well as cracking in the wood itself.

The solutions to these two problems are relatively simple. Avoid placing furniture in strong sunlight and try to keep relative humidity (RH) within a tolerable range. While precise RH control is not usually within the capabilities of most homeowners, you should try to avoid moving furniture from a very cold location to a hot location (RH drops as the air is heated). Avoid prolonged storage of furniture in hot locations like attics or damp locations like basements. Do not place furniture close to radiators or near vents that blow hot air directly onto the surface of the furniture.

## Maintaining Finish Appearance

Routine maintenance of the surface does not halt the ravages of time, but it will prevent an unattractive buildup of dirt and grime. Waxing, polishing, and dusting help maintain an attractive appearance and lend a pleasing, tactile quality to the surface finish.

### WAXING

A coat of paste wax on top of a finish provides a thin layer of protection against abrasions and other superficial damage. Most paste waxes are formulated from carnauba, beeswax, and paraffin wax. Carnauba gives the wax hardness and shine, beeswax is softer and has a more satiny appearance, and paraffin makes the wax easy to apply. These three waxes are liquefied and mixed with a mineral-spirits carrier to put the wax into a paste form. Pigments and dyes may be added to color the wax (see the photo on p. 166). Generally, colored waxes are used on dark wood and natural waxes on light wood. Colored waxes should always be used on dark woods with open pores; if you use a natural color, the wax that remains in the pores dries to a light color, which may be objectionable.

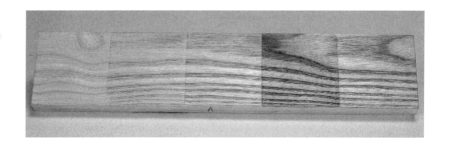

**Natural waxes (left) tone down the pore structure, while colored waxes accentuate it, as shown on this ash sample board.**

Wax can be applied full strength or thinned. When used full strength, wax can be difficult to apply evenly, so it's best to make an applicator pad. Place a generous chunk of the wax in the center of a 10-in. square piece of cotton cloth and fold the corners of the pad over to cover the wax, as shown in the top two photos on the facing page. (If you prefer to apply wax with a rag, thin the wax 50/50 with mineral spirits or naphtha.) Wipe the wax on evenly in any direction you wish and, when it hazes over, buff to a satin sheen with a clean, dry cloth. For a higher gloss, you can let the wax dry longer, and polish it with a lamb's-wool buffer. Reapply the wax once or twice a year.

Once you have wax on the surface, periodic dusting is easy. Use a damp cloth to remove the dust, and then take a clean cloth and buff to restore the appearance. Wax does not build up significantly, as you may have been led to believe. The only time wax should be removed is when it has a lot of dust in it or when it smudges badly when you try to buff it. In this case, remove the wax with naphtha or mineral spirits (you don't need to buy special wax removers). You can use 0000 steel wool with the mineral spirits to speed up the process.

Colored waxes can be used to add subtle decorative effects. On woods with prominent pores, the wax can add a decorative highlight, as long as you haven't filled the pores with paste-wood filler. Dark wax can be left in corners for antiquing. You can make your own colored waxes by adding pigment or oil-soluble dye to natural wax.

The only problem I've encountered with commercial waxes is with the carrier. Some waxes (such as Briwax) use toluene as the carrier, which can remove oil finishes and soften other finishes like lacquer if left on the surface too long. These waxes should be used with discretion on newly finished pieces. On completely cured finishes, they work fine.

To make a wax-polishing pad, place a chunk of wax in the center of a piece of cotton cloth.

Fold the corners over to form the pad.

Apply the wax in an even coat, using a circular motion. Buff with a clean, dry cloth as soon as the wax starts to haze.

## POLISHING

Polishes are liquids that are used to clean the finish and to restore shine temporarily. They are either oil based, like lemon-oil, or oil/water emulsions. These products contain little or no wax. They are usually slow-evaporating oily solvents with mineral or silicone oil to produce a longer-lasting surface luster on the wood. While touted as conditioners and restoration products, the luster and shine that polishes produce do not last very long because the components eventually evaporate.

The best use of polishes is to remove dirt, grease, and oils. Oil/water polishes clean both oil-soluble dirt (oils from our skin) and water-soluble dirt like food spills. Polishes should be applied more often than wax because they do not form a surface coating.

If you read older antique-restoration books or go to antique stores, you may come across finish "revivers." These polishes are mixtures of linseed oil, turpentine (mineral spirits), and sometimes vinegar. The vinegar and mineral-spirits combination cleans different types of dirt as explained above, but the linseed oil can cause problems. If linseed oil is left on the surface of a film-forming finish like shellac, lacquer, or varnish, it will never dry to a hard film. It will remain sticky and gummy and become a dust and dirt magnet; it will also become extremely difficult to remove. This is exactly the opposite of what you want a polish to do. Linseed oil and any other drying oils in polishes should be used only over oil finishes, and they should be applied very thinly.

## Cleaning Finishes

When dirt and oils are not routinely removed by cleaning and are allowed to build up, they can be difficult to clean. Many years of neglect may result in a surface that looks as though it will require stripping, but in many cases a thorough cleaning will be enough to restore the surface. Since the buildup of grime is from various types of dirt, a two-step cleaning process works best.

The first step is to remove the oil-soluble wax and oils from the surface. Use mineral spirits or naphtha on a clean rag and wipe the surface, working in small circles. Move to a fresh area of the rag to expose clean cloth. If the surface is very dirty, use very fine steel wool in conjunction with the solvent to help cut through the dirt. Go easy because you will abrade a little of the finish when doing this. Afterwards, wipe the surface with a clean cloth. When the surface is dry, seal any bare wood areas with a sealer coat of shellac to prevent grain raising in the next step. To remove the water-soluble dirt, use a grease-cutting dishwashing detergent dissolved in warm water. Use about a capful per pint. Work the surface in small circles with a rag that's slightly damp, not dripping wet, and wipe the dirt/slurry off with a clean cloth before it dries. Remove any detergent residue with a clean, water-dampened cloth.

As long as there is enough finish left on the surface, a simple rewaxing with several applications of paste wax should result in an attractive finish. If the finish is missing in certain areas, or you want to build up more finish, reapply the finish of your choice. It's a good idea to scuff-sand the surface with 240-grit sandpaper to provide a mechanical bond between the old and new finish. Lacquer, shellac, and most varnishes adhere well to old surfaces. I do not recommend using polyurethane because it does not bond well.

## Repairing Finishes

Over time, furniture acquires various scratches, dents, gouges, and other forms of wear and tear. While some minor defects can be tolerated, other blemishes disfigure the overall appearance of a piece of furniture and should be repaired.

### SCRATCHES

Scratches can be repaired in a variety of ways, depending on the type of finish and the severity of the scratch. The easiest way to make a temporary repair to any superficial, minor scratch or to light scratching that causes dullness over the entire surface is to wipe on some polish or rewax the finish. For dark woods, use dark polish or colored waxes; for light woods, use a natural-colored wax. A more permanent repair is to remove the scratch by abrading it or filling it with more finish.

*Oil finishes*    Minor scratches in oil finishes can be repaired by wiping on some of the original finish. If the scratch is deep and has cut into the wood, you should sand out the scratch and refinish the whole area with more stain and finish. If it's a large surface like a dining-room table and the scratch is small, then fill the scratch with a wax stick of the appropriate color (see pp. 171-172).

*Film finishes*    Scratches that are in the surface finish of lacquer, varnish, or shellac can be sanded out as long as the finish is thick enough. The technique for making this repair is just like rubbing out a finish (see pp. 126-130). Start with the finest-grit wet/dry paper that will remove the scratch (I recommend starting with 600 to be safe). Clean the surface with naphtha first, and then wet-sand the scratched area and feather it out into the rest of the finish. Then progress through the rubbing-out process, using finer abrasives until you reach the sheen that you want. It's important to rub out the entire surface, since concentrating your efforts only in the damaged area will make it look slightly different from the rest of the surface, especially on flat surfaces when viewed in backlighting.

Some finishes are too thin to sand out the scratch completely, or you may feel nervous about sanding scratches on a finish that you are unsure of. The best way to repair scratches in this case is just the opposite of the technique described on p. 169: Fill the scratches by applying more finish or, if you don't know what the finish is, use a padding lacquer. Shellac and solvent-based lacquer repair the best because these finishes redissolve when more of the original finish is applied. Varnish and water-based lacquer are more problematic, and the repair may be slightly visible. To determine which finish you have, try a series of simple tests. Pick an inconspicuous area and dab some alcohol on it. Wait one minute; if the finish is sticky, it's shellac. If not, repeat with lacquer thinner. If the finish gets sticky now, it's solvent lacquer or possibly water-based lacquer. (Not all water-based finishes will be affected by lacquer thinner.) If neither solvent works, the finish is an oil, a varnish, or a water-based finish.

Clean the surface of all old waxes and polishes with naphtha before applying more finish or padding lacquer. It's up to you which finish you use. Shellac, of course, works best over shellac, but it can be applied over any other finish without adhesion problems. Padding lacquer has a variety of solvents in it which redissolve shellac, lacquer, and some water-based lacquers. Varnishes do not redissolve, but as long as the scratches are fresh and not too deep, the padding lacquer will cover up the damage without much visibility.

Padding lacquer is applied differently depending on the depth of the scratches. If scratches are deep, you may first want to fill them partially by applying some padding lacquer with an artist's brush

**If a scratch is deep, apply finish to the scratch with an artist's brush before refinishing the entire surface.**

just to the scratch (see the photo on the facing page). After allowing the repair to dry for about an hour, you can proceed to apply the padding lacquer as explained in Chapter 7.

If the scratches are not too deep and the finish is lacquer or shellac, a faster way to remove scratches is to use a quick-drying padding lacquer like Star's Lac-French or Mohawk's Quick Pad. Make a pad by wadding up some padding cloth, being careful to avoid seams or wrinkles on the bottom. Pour a small amount of padding lacquer on the bottom and tap it against your palm to distribute the lacquer throughout the pad. Glide the pad down onto the surface and quickly buff back and forth in a pendulum-like motion. Use light pressure at first, and then gradually increase the pressure. Work briskly and never let the pad stop on the surface. What you're doing is a combination of redissolving the finish and filling the scratches. The strong solvents in these lacquers dry quickly, so the finish is dry to the touch and can be handled immediately. The padding process makes a satin finish glossy; if you want to reduce the sheen, wait until the lacquer has dried hard enough to rub out with steel wool. Wait a day or so before placing anything on the refinished surfaces.

### DENTS AND GOUGES
Dents and gouges in the finish can be handled with similar materials, but the technique varies depending on the type of damage.

***Small gouges and nail holes***  Small defects are best handled with colored wax sticks, which are sold by Star, Mohawk, and Behlen. The sticks, which are nothing more than hard wax with pigment, are available in a variety of tones. You can rub the stick over a small

To fill a small gouge, press some wax into the gouge and then use a wooden "chisel" to scrape off the excess wax flush with the surrounding finish.

**Use the smooth paper side of a piece of sandpaper to smooth the wax to the level of the surrounding finish.**

gouge or nail hole to fill the defect, and then scrape off the excess with a cloth. However, this technique can create a visible shallow spot in the wax, so I recommend an alternative method. Push some wax into the gouge and press it down with a small wooden "chisel" (a block of wood with a beveled end). Then scrape off the bulk of the excess wax (see the photo on p. 171). Next smooth the wax with the paper side of a piece of fine sandpaper, as shown in the photo above. Using the smooth side of the paper levels the wax only to the surface of the surrounding finish, avoiding the problem of the shallow spot around the repair. If the color isn't quite right, rub one color over another to change the shade. As long as the defect is small, most finishes can be applied over the wax, but shellac and padding lacquer work best.

**Large dents and gouges** Because wax is soft, it doesn't provide much protection against wear and tear. For larger dents and gouges, or for a more durable repair, the best filler material is shellac sticks. These sticks are composed of colored shellac or lacquer resins. The sticks melt at a low enough temperature that they can be applied to the defect without damaging the surrounding finish. The process is called *burning in*.

Professionals who do a lot of burning in use an electric oven and specially designed knives that can apply and then level the burn-in material without damaging the finish. This can be an expensive way to go if you only do occasional burn-ins, so I will discuss an easier method. For this method you need shellac-based sticks, which are made by Mohawk, Behlen, and M.L. Campbell. The method doesn't work with lacquer-based sticks such as those made by Star.

Pick a color stick that is slightly lighter than the lightest background color of the wood. On natural finishes or when the damage

# Repairing a Gouge

1. To repair a large gouge, melt some stick shellac with a hot electric burn-in knife.

2. Press the hot shellac into the gouge with the tip of the knife.

3. Push down on the shellac with your finger before it cools.

4. Using a muslin-wrapped, cork-faced block wetted with alcohol and naphtha, rub the repaired area flush with the finish.

5. Wet-sand the repair with 600-grit wet/dry sandpaper, using naphtha as a lubricant.

6. Paint in fine grain lines to complete the repair.

is only to the clear finish, use clear or amber-colored sticks. Using an electric burn-in knife or a soldering pencil, melt the tip of the stick and press it into the defect (see the photos on p. 173). Push down on the shellac with the tip of your finger to force out any air bubbles. Next wrap some muslin or other cotton cloth around a cork-faced block. Make a solution of one part denatured alcohol and one part naphtha and wet the cloth with some of the solution. Now rub the burn-in area, working at it from all angles until the repair is almost level. The alcohol removes the high spots of the shellac without damaging the finish surrounding it. To complete the repair, wet-sand with 600-grit wet/dry sandpaper, using naphtha as a lubricant. On thin finishes, use your hand to back the paper; on thicker finishes you can use a block.

This technique works best with finishes that are impervious to alcohol, such as lacquer and varnish. If you're careful, you can use the same technique with shellac finishes, but the alcohol will probably remove some of the surrounding finish so you may want to try wet-sanding the shellac stick with naphtha only.

Whatever the finish, the repaired area will probably still be slightly visible, so you should adjust the color and paint in grain lines. This is best done with dry pigment powders (see p. 64) mixed with shellac. Using a fine-tipped artist's brush, mix some pigment to paint in the darker grain lines, and then adjust the color of the burn-in, if necessary. Painting in the grain lines darkens the overall shade of the shellac stick, so you may find this step unnecessary. I usually paint the grain lines first, and then adjust the shade of the burn-in by mixing very light washes of pigment and shellac. I proceed very slowly, adjusting the shade carefully and looking at the repair from various angles to make sure it doesn't go too dark. Repaired areas that are lighter tend to be less visible than dark repairs, so I usually try to avoid the temptation to get the repair perfect. Working in natural daylight is best for this work. Once you're satisfied with the color, let the repair dry several hours, and then pad some shellac or padding lacquer over the whole area. This step isn't absolutely necessary, but it does provide a clear lens under which the repair is almost invisible. Applying the shellac or padding lacquer also helps to protect the repaired area.

**WATER RINGS AND HEAT RINGS**

Water rings show up as white spots in the finish. They are easiest to repair on finishes that redissolve in their own solvent, like lacquer or shellac. Simply wipe the affected area with an alcohol-dampened rag and the white spot will disappear. Varnish is harder to eradicate completely. The best approach with this finish is to abrade the finish with some fine steel wool and mineral spirits. You can also use an automotive rubbing compound. In extreme cases, 600-grit wet/dry paper will work, followed by rubbing back up to the desired sheen.

Heat rings are more problematic. Mild heat rings can sometimes be eradicated by wet-sanding until the white marks are gone. Severe heat marks that go all the way through the film can only be repaired by stripping and refinishing.

## ABRASIONS

Edges or sharp corners that have missing color as a result of an abrasion can be repaired by replacing the color with a dye and then top-coating with a clear finish. An alternative technique is to paint the missing color with a blend of pigment and shellac (see the photo below). Either technique will work, but it's best to use the same technique that was used in the original finishing process. If the abrasion hasn't gone completely through to bare wood, use an alcohol dye so that it will "bite" into the remaining finish. On large areas that are rubbed completely through to the bare wood, using a water dye takes only to the exposed wood, which is a real benefit if you're not skilled with an artist's brush.

## SURFACE MARKS

Any residue that lies on the surface of the wood may initially appear to be a gouge or a scratch. White paint picked up from walls when moving furniture almost always looks like a deep scratch at first. These surface marks can be removed with the appropriate solvent and rubbing. For glue marks and scuff marks, mineral spirits usually works. For latex-paint marks, use warm water and fine steel wool. Oil paint requires mineral spirits and steel wool.

**To repair an abraded edge, paint the abrasion with shellac tinted with pigment or alcohol-soluble dye.**

# Glossary

**Acrylic** A resin used in lacquer formulations that is hard, tough, and clear (Plexiglas is an example). Acrylics are favored for their stain resistance and nonyellowing characteristics.

**Alkyd** A synthetic resin of great importance in finishing products. Made by reacting an alcohol with an acid (al-cid = alkyd).

**Aniline** A chemical that was one of the principal starting ingredients in the early manufacture of dyes. Aniline is still used to denote a class of dye stains used in wood, textile, and leather finishing.

**Binder** A substance used in finishing products to bind or attach pigment particles to one another and to the wood. Synonymous terms are vehicle, medium, and resin.

**Bleeding** The migration of a colorant into the finishing material, which causes a muddy, opaque appearance.

**Blushing** The tendency of finishes applied in high humidity to turn white, or blush, when moisture is trapped within the film as it dries.

**Bodying** The second stage in French polishing, in which the shellac is built up after the pores are filled.

**Burn-in** A term used to describe the fusing of finish layers between application. Solvent-release finishes like shellac and solvent lacquer have 100% burn-in. Water-based finishes vary in burn-in from around 20% to none at all. Reactive finishes like varnish do not burn in at all. Burn-in is a desirable quality in finishes that are rubbed out. Also used to describe a method of applying stick shellac to a repair, a process called burning in.

**Carrier** A liquid in finishing products that enables the product to be applied to the wood evenly. The carrier always evaporates and is no longer present when the product is fully cured. Common carriers are mineral spirits, alcohol, and water.

**Casein** The principal protein in milk. It is produced by reacting skim milk with an acid that forms curds. When the curds are washed in water and then dried, the resulting substance is casein. Casein is used in the manufacture of milk paint.

**Chemical stains** Chemicals that react with other chemicals naturally present in the wood to produce a color change. Common chemicals are potassium dichromate, sodium hydroxide, and ammonia.

**Clearing** The final stage in French polishing, in which the residual oil used during the finishing process is removed.

**Coalescing solvent** A solvent in water-based finishes that dissolves the resin. It is present in small amounts to keep the resin "sticky" enough so that it will form a smooth, contiguous film when dry. Coalescing solvents are members of the glycol-ether family of solvents.

**Colloidal suspension** A mixture of a fine powder in a liquid.

**Crackle** Mechanically imitating *craquelure* on finishes. Craquelure is the pattern of fine cracks that appears in finishes as they age (also known as crazing).

**Cut** The ratio of dry shellac flakes in pounds dissolved in a gallon of alcohol. For example, 2 lb. of shellac dissolved in one gallon of alcohol is a 2-lb. cut; 5 lb. is a 5-lb. cut.

**Cyanoacrylate** A fast-drying, waterproof glue sold under brand names like Krazy Glue, Super Glue, and Hot Stuff.

**Defoamer** A substance added to water-based finishes to reduce the foaming caused by the surfactants in the formulation.

**Denatured alcohol** Ethanol that has chemicals added to it to make it unfit for human consumption.

**Diluent** A neutral solvent used to bulk up the volume of thinners.

**Distressing** Mechanically damaging a piece of furniture to imitate natural wear and tear.

**Drier** A chemical that is added to reactive oil-based finishes to hasten the uptake of oxygen and so speed the cure time.

**Dye** A chemical that is dissolved in a medium to impart color. Because the colored particles are so small, they absorb and transmit light, which make dyes transparent. *See also* Pigments.

**Earth pigments** A class of pigments that occur naturally as minerals and are mined from the earth. Sometimes referred to as iron oxides.

**Emulsion** A mixture of two substances that normally do not mix, such as oil and water. Emulsifiers are chemicals that force these substances to be dispersed evenly.

**Esterification** A chemical equilibrium reaction between an organic acid and an alcohol. Esterification is the chemical process that eventually renders shellac gummy after it is dissolved in alcohol.

**Esters** A class of solvents that includes ethyl acetate and butyl acetate. Esters are solvents for lacquer resin.

**Fish-eye** A crater that forms in a finish as a result of surface-tension disparities between the liquid finish and contaminants in the pores of the wood.

**Flags** A term in brush manufacture used to denote splits at the very tip of the bristle. Flags are naturally occurring on natural bristle like hog hair and mechanically produced on synthetic filaments.

**Flattener** An inert, translucent powder such as silica added to gloss finishes to reduce the sheen by deflecting light away from the eye.

**Flowout** The desirable property of a finish that applies evenly and forms a smooth, contiguous film as it dries.

**French polishing** A method of applying shellac by hand in thin layers with a cloth pad.

**Fresco powder** A very finely ground dry pigment.

**Fugitive** A term used to describe colors that are prone to fading in light.

**Gelling agent** An inert substance added to finishing products to make them thixotropic. This means that the product remains in a gelled state until energy is applied (by wiping or brushing), which converts it to a liquid state.

**Gel stain** A stain that has been thickened to improve handling.

**Glaze** Color applied between coats of clear finish.

**Glycol ethers** A class of solvents that find use in finishing products because of their compatibility with a wide variety of products. The most common are sold under the Cellosolve trade name. They are used as lacquer retarders, water-based resin solvents, and in NGR stain formulations.

**Hide glue** A natural glue made by processing cattle hides. It is usually sold in dry granules, which are soaked in water and then heated. Liquid hide glue is made from the dry granules and water, but special antigelling agents are added to prevent the glue from hardening in the bottle.

**Hydrocarbons** A class of solvents that are made up of hydrogen and carbon. They are further subdivided into aliphatic hydrocarbons (those based upon a straight carbon chain) and aromatic hydrocarbons (those based upon a ring structure). Hydrocarbon solvents are miscible with oil and oil-based products like linseed oil.

**Hygrometer** A device used to measure relative humidity.

**Japan colors** Finely ground pigments in an oil/varnish binder. Unlike oil paints, they dry to a flat luster because of the high ratio of pigment.

**Ketones** A class of solvents that includes acetone and methyl ethyl ketone. Ketones are solvents for lacquer resins.

**Lacquer** A type of finish that dries primarily by solvent evaporation.

**Lightfastness** The resistance of colored compounds to the fading action produced by light.

**Linseed oil** A drying oil made from the seeds of the flax plant.

**Long-oil varnish** A varnish manufactured with a high percentage of a drying oil, which increases the flexibility for exterior use. Sometimes called marine or spar varnish.

**Milk paint** A paint made from casein dissolved in lime and water to which natural earth pigments are added.

**Mineral spirits** A generic name used to classify a range of solvents that are mixtures of aliphatic and aromatic hydrocarbon solvents. Mineral spirits with no aromatic hydrocarbons are known as odorless mineral spirits.

**Naphtha** A blend of aliphatic and aromatic hydrocarbons used to thin oil-based paints and finishes. This flammable solvent is also a good cleaner for dirty finishes and removes wax. The most commonly sold version is called VM&P (varnish maker's and painter's) naphtha.

**Nitrocellulose** A term used to denote resins based on cellulose nitrate. Technically, nitrocellulose is an incorrect term because the resin contains no nitro groups, but the term has stuck.

**Non-grain-raising (NGR) stain** A catch-all term that is applied to a premixed dye stain in a volatile solvent that will not raise the grain of the wood.

**Open time** The amount of time a finishing medium remains manipulable. Also applies to glues.

**Oxidized oil** A drying oil heated in the presence of air to temperatures around 570°F.

**Paste-wood filler** A product designed to fill in the pore cavities in wood so that a smooth surface finish can be obtained. It can be oil or water based and is comprised of a bulking agent (silex), binder, carrier, and pigment (for colored fillers).

**Phenolic resin** A hard, tough resin used in oil-varnish manufacturing. Useful in exterior applications and where good rubbing qualities are desired.

**Pigment** A fine, colored powder insoluble in the medium in which it is applied. The size of pigment particles makes them absorb and reflect light, which renders them opaque. *See also* Dyes.

**Plasticizer** A chemical added to finishes to keep them flexible over time.

**Polymerization** A chemical process in which smaller molecules (monomers) link up to form larger molecules (polymers). Oils cure by a polymerizing process called auto-oxidative polymerization. The smaller oil molecules react with oxygen, which forms a larger molecule that is harder.

**Polymerized oil** A drying oil heated in the absence of air to temperatures around 485°F to 570°F.

**Polyurethane** A durable finishing medium based on urethane.

**Polyvinyl acetate (PVA)** The main resin used in wood glues like Titebond and Elmer's.

**Pressure-sensitive adhesive (PSA)** An adhesive used on the back of sandpaper to provide a means of attachment to a machine sander.

**Pumice** Very fine volcanic glass, used as a polishing abrasive in rubbing out finishes and as a pore filler in French polishing.

**Reactive finish** A finish that cures by a reactive chemical process, usually polymerization. Oils and varnishes are reactive finishes because the cured film formed is a reaction product between the drying oil and oxygen in the air.

**Relative humidity (RH)** The amount of moisture in the air expressed as a percentage of the amount of moisture that the air is capable of holding at that temperature.

**Resin** A broad term applied to synthetic or natural organic polymers that form the hard part of a finish when it dries.

**Retarder** A slow-evaporating solvent compatible with the finishing product added to increase the drying time.

**Rottenstone** A polishing abrasive based on fine, decomposed limestone. Generally used to bring a finish to final gloss.

**Rubbing compound** An abrasive compound made into a paste that is used to smooth and polish a clear finish.

**Rubbing out** A process used to level imperfections, smooth the surface, and establish a consistent sheen to a clear finish.

**Sanding schedule** A term used to designate the grit progression in preparing a piece of furniture for finishing.

**Shelf life** The amount of time that the manufacturer guarantees a finishing product will remain useful.

**Shellac** The alcohol-soluble resin produced by the lac insect. It is sold in a wide variety of grades such as buttonlac, sticklac, seedlac, #1 orange, and super-blonde.

**Short-oil varnish** A varnish manufactured with a low percentage of drying-oil vehicle, which increases the hardness to make rubbing out easier.

**Solids content** The amount of resin/vehicle in a clear finish expressed as a percentage of the total volume of the finish.

**Solvent** Any liquid that is capable of dissolving a resin or other type of solid.

**Solvent-release finish** A finish that dries (forms a film) by evaporation of its solvent carrier. The dried film does not undergo a chemical change (polymerize) so the finish will always redissolve in its original carrier solvent. Shellac and solvent lacquer are the best examples of these finishes.

**Spar varnish** An exterior, long-oil varnish usually based on tung-oil-modified phenolic resin.

**Spirit varnish** An older type of varnish made by dissolving natural resins like sandarac and dammar in alcohol (spirit). Shellac is sometimes referred to as a spirit varnish in older texts.

**Splotching** Uneven stain penetration caused by changes in wood density.

**Stain** A product that imparts a color change to wood without obscuring the grain and figure.

**Stearate** A catch-all term that usually refers to zinc stearate, a chemical added to sandpaper to reduce clogging. Stearate is also added to sanding sealers to promote easy sanding of the dried sealer. It is sometimes used as a flattening agent.

**Stick shellac** A repair product made from resin colored with dyes and/or pigments. Some modern versions use nitrocellulose resin, others still use shellac.

**Surface tension** The contractile force present in liquids that causes them to assume a spherical shape when in contact with another surface. Water beading on glass is caused by a strong disparity between the surface tension of water (high) and that of glass (low).

**Surfactant (surface-active agent)** Any compound that reduces surface tension between two liquids or a liquid and a solid. Soap is a common surfactant. Surfactants are also known as wetting agents.

**Tannin** A substance that is present in varying amounts in all woods. It reacts with some chemicals like ammonia to produce coloring changes in the wood.

**Tipping off** A technique used in brushing varnish to smooth out irregularities in the wet varnish by lightly dragging the tip of a brush across the finish at a 90° angle to the surface.

**Tung oil** A drying oil made from the tung nut. Sometimes called china wood oil.

**Universal tinting colors (UTCs)** Pigments ground into a water/glycol ether/acrylic base. They can be used in most finishing products.

**Urethane** A resin used in finishes and stains. Pure urethane is rarely used; most often it is modified with an alkyd and known as a uralkyd. Nonetheless, urethane or polyurethane is usually the marketed name.

**Varnish** A thin protective coating used on wood based upon drying oil as the vehicle.

**Volatile organic compounds (VOCs)** Evaporative chemicals, usually fast-evaporating hydrocarbon solvents, responsible for smog and poor air quality. Restricting the amount of these solvents in finishing products has been mandated in many states.

**Wash coat** A very thinned finish applied to fresh wood to control stain application.

**Water-based finish** A broad term applied to those finishes in which a flammable and hazardous carrier is replaced by water.

**Whiting** Calcium carbonate or chalk. Sold in various degrees of fineness.

**Witness line** A visible line created in finishes that do not fuse to each other when rubbing out.

# Index

**Publisher:** JAMES P. CHIAVELLI

**Acquisitions Editor:** RICK PETERS

**Publishing Coordinator:** JOANNE RENNA

**Editor:** PETER CHAPMAN

**Layout Artist:** AMY L. BERNARD

**Photographer:** ERNIE CONOVER

**Illustrator:** MIKE WANKE

**Typeface:** PLANTIN

**Paper:** WARREN PATINA MATTE, 70 lb., NEUTRAL pH

**Printer:** QUEBECOR PRINTING/HAWKINS, NEW CANTON, TENNESSEE